Your Quick & Easy
Car Care and
Safe Driving Handbook

Your Quick & Easy Car Care and Safe Driving Handbook

LAURA FLYNN McCARTHY

Illustrations by Edward R. Lipinski

Doubleday

New York   London   Toronto   Sydney   Auckland

PUBLISHED BY DOUBLEDAY
a division of Bantam Doubleday Dell Publishing Group, Inc.
666 Fifth Avenue, New York, New York 10103

DOUBLEDAY and the portrayal of an anchor
with a dolphin are trademarks of Doubleday,
a division of Bantam Doubleday Dell Publishing
Group, Inc.

Author's Note: This book was put together with the invaluable assistance of automotive engineer John Fobian, to whom I give great thanks. Some suggestions on negotiating new- and used-car deals were provided by consumer advocate Jack Gillis. Very special thanks go to my husband, Kevin, and all of my family for their unfailing support.

Doubleday and the author have made every reasonable effort to ensure the accuracy and reliability of the general information, instructions, and directions in this book. However, it is sold with the understanding that Doubleday and the author are engaged in rendering no more than general guidance. If expert advice is needed for your particular automobile problem, you must obtain the services of a professional in the field who can evaluate your specific circumstance. Doubleday and the author specifically disclaim any personal liability for misinterpretation of the directions, human error, typographical mistakes or other loss or risk incurred as a consequence of the advice or information presented herein.

Library of Congress Cataloging-in-Publication Data

McCarthy, Laura Flynn.
    Your quick & easy car care and safe driving handbook/Laura Flynn McCarthy. p. cm.
    1. Automobiles—Handbooks, manuals, etc. 2. Automobile driving—Handbooks, manuals, etc.   I. Title. II. Title: Your quick and easy car care and safe driving handbook.
TL151.M366   1990
629.28'722—dc20

89-28150
CIP

ISBN 0-385-40003-9

Contents

Foreword

Few possessions play as important a role in day-to-day living as the automobile. After you've owned one for a little while, you can't *imagine* how you ever survived without it. Your automobile is most likely the way you get to work each day, where you load up your weekly groceries, the means by which you vacation each year, and, if you're like many people, one of your sources of greatest pride. In an era when cars cost as much as a house might have twenty years ago, your automobile is also probably one of the heftiest investments you'll make in your lifetime. All of these are reasons why car owners today need—and want—to be more informed about their prize possessions than ever before.

Today's automobile is a completely different machine than the first combustion-engine automobile invented by Carl Benz in 1885. The introduction of modern devices—computers that can set your ignition timing or create a dashboard voice that reminds you to buckle your seat belt; turbochargers to rev up an already superior engine; fuel-injection; multicylinders—all combine to form one of the most sophisticated machines money can buy. While today's cars can do things that Henry Ford probably never dreamed of, the high technology involved also makes them much more complicated to repair—one of the reasons why the experts who correct malfunctions in today's cars are sometimes called "technicians" rather than "mechanics."

Yet, even with today's complicated engines, most car owners aren't as helpless as they think they are. Many men and women rely on auto mechanics when they really don't need to. The key to a smooth-running, *reliable* automobile is in regular, careful maintenance, comprised of steps that anyone can do— from checking the oil once a week to taking the car in for a tune-up every 10,000 miles. If you have time to read only one chapter in this book, make it chapter one, "Maintenance: Keeping Your Car in Peak Performance." Follow the steps outlined there, and in the maintenance timetable in the back of this book, and you could save hundreds of dollars and hours of anguish by preventing costly repairs.

Good preventive action also means knowing the best ways to drive your car to keep it in top running order. In chapter five you'll find driving tactics pertaining to a variety of weather conditions (from a snowstorm to a steaming hot day) and stressful situations (such as when your car overheats). For a simple, basic understanding of how your car operates, turn to chapter two, and then the following chapter, in which you'll learn about your car's trouble signs and what to do about them. Since even the most "babied" cars occasionally need professional attention, this book has a separate chapter on ways to find a reliable mechanic. And when it comes time to turn your "Old Faithful" in for a newer model, the last chapters will instruct you on strategies for buying a new or used car and how to keep it insured without depleting your bank account.

This book is written and designed for you to keep handy in your glove compartment, right beside your car owner's manual. It should serve both as a ready resource for emergency situations (such as when you have to change a flat tire) and less dire, but still stressful encounters (such as when you have to outtalk a car dealer or sort through options offered by insurance plans).

You don't have to be a mechanic to drive a car, and you won't find any terms in this book that can't be understood easily by any licensed driver—young or old, male or female, diehard auto buff or first-time car owner. This is a book designed to make you a better driver and a more informed car owner, and that means safer traveling for everyone on the road.

1
Maintenance: Keeping Your Car in Peak Performance

The term "maintenance" means different things to different people. For some, it's just a simple matter of keeping the gas tank full and having the car tuned up once a year. But, to keep your car running in peak performance, maintenance also means making a quick one-minute checkup of your car every time you drive, and more detailed weekly and monthly checkups; keeping tabs on all fluid levels, on tire pressure, balance, and alignment; washing your car regularly, inside and out; and taking care of repairs as soon as they arise—not after they've had a chance to disrupt a system that's working well. In short, maintenance means keeping "tuned in" to how your automobile runs.

Before you begin the "what-to-dos" and "where-to-look-fors" of regular car maintenance, take some time to think about safety.

Unless otherwise noted, all of the maintenance checks described in this chapter are performed with the car parked on level ground and the engine turned *off*. Running engine parts can pose all sorts of hazards; even in situations where a proper check requires that the engine be on (such as when checking transmission fluid), make sure to work *only* with the engine part described in the check, and don't touch any other part.

Remove any objects that could get in your way: if you have long hair, tie it back; if you are wearing a necktie, tuck it inside your shirt; if you wear jewelry, remove it. In fair weather, if you're wearing an oversized shirt, tuck it into your jeans or overalls. During the winter, zip up your extra long scarf *inside* your coat so that it won't accidentally get stuck or sucked up in an engine part.

Never smoke or light a match when you're checking under your car's hood.

Maintaining an automobile is not a dangerous job; in fact, driving a poorly maintained vehicle is much *more* dangerous. But you should work carefully and systematically when making checkups or repairs on your own. Giving your automobile regular checkups is important, but only if you know what to look for. On the following pages you'll find guidelines on how to recognize wear-and-tear on tires; how to check and add oil and other fluids; what to look for when examining hoses, belts, and your air filter; how to check—and change—radiator fluid; ways to examine some of the components of your exhaust and suspension systems; how to test your battery; and even tips for doing the best job possible when washing and waxing your car. Once you know how to examine your car, you can follow the chart on pages 186–88 as a quick-reference guide to keep your car in the best possible condition.

THE WELL-EQUIPPED TRUNK AND GLOVE COMPARTMENT

Being a knowledgeable driver means keeping your car well stocked and prepared for any situation. It's never a good idea to load up your trunk with *too* much heavy gear, as added weight can put unnecessary stress on an engine. But, some equipment should be standard inventory for any trunk or glove compartment year-round. Here are lists of items that smart drivers should never be without.

TRUNK:
☐ Tool kit, including screwdriver, hammer, pliers, cross-type lug wrench for changing a tire, extra lug nuts for wheels, extra valve caps for tires, extra hose clamps to reattach a loosened radiator hose until you can have it replaced permanently.

☐ Jack and spare tire (standard equipment on any new car; should be included in any used car deal, too).

☐ Emergency equipment, including first aid kit; fire-resistant blanket; emergency flares and/or reflecting signs; fire extinguisher.

☐ Pair of eye goggles and a pair of flexible protective gloves to protect eyes and hands from dangers such as scalding water bursting up from a radiator if the engine overheats or sparks being set off by electrical wires.

☐ Battery booster (jumper) cables for recharging a battery.

☐ A gallon each of windshield wiper fluid, and antifreeze/coolant, and a quart of engine oil.

☐ Spare windshield wiper blades.

☐ Multipurpose rags or paper towels.

☐ For a list of special equipment to add to your trunk just before winter, see pages 122–23.

Do not store gasoline in your trunk. While having extra gas in your trunk used to be considered good standard prevention, the risks of an explosion set off by a rear-end collision with another car outweigh any advantages.

GLOVE COMPARTMENT:
☐ Notepad and working pen or pencil.

☐ Flashlight with working batteries.

☐ Change to make an emergency phone call.

☐ Auto insurance card, registration, and required inspection certificates. (If you live in an area of high auto theft, carry these cards on your person, rather than in your car. A thief could use these documents to impersonate you when confronted by police or other authorities.)

☐ Phone numbers of 24-hour tow service and/or emergency numbers for the auto club to which you belong.

☐ Good, clear road maps of anywhere you plan to travel.

☐ Tire pressure gauge; tread-wear gauge.

KEEPING YOUR CAR CLEAN

Washing and waxing your car regularly not only exhibits your pride as a car owner, but it may also be the cheapest, easiest way to sustain a high value at trade-in or resale time.

Dirt and salt from the road, rain and snow, tree sap, bird droppings, even smoggy air can cause your car to age much sooner than it has to. You should wash your car once a week (including removing any interior clutter) and wax it at least twice a year.

Start off by attending to your car's interior. Shortly after you buy a new car, it's a good idea to spray upholstered seats with a fabric sealant (such as Scotchguard). For cleaning vinyl car seats, use a gentle silicone spray or an all-purpose cleaner whose label specifies that it's for vinyl and plastic surfaces. Take care of any spots immediately with a spot remover. Install floor mats to protect carpeting. Vacuum seats and carpeting at least once a month. Keep a few plastic "trash bags" handy to collect loose scraps of paper and refuse.

Car-washing Tips

☐ If your car has recently had a paint job or body work, wait at least a week (maybe as long as a month) to wash your car, in order to give the paint plenty of time to set.

☐ Park your car out of direct sunlight. Use a mild soap such as dishwashing liquid (harsher detergents could spot the finish) in a mixture of one tablespoon to a gallon of warm water. First, hose down your car with lukewarm water, then apply the soapy mixture with a large soft sponge, hosing each area quickly so that the soap doesn't dry and form a film. Work from the top of your car, beginning with the roof, to the bottom, so that dirty water won't spill down on areas as you clean them.

□ For hard-to-remove stains like bird droppings, tar or oil from the road, or tree sap, either concentrate more of your own "elbow grease" and soap mixture on the particular spot, or use cleaning solvents available at auto parts stores especially prepared for car bodies. Don't use harsh detergents, steel wool pads, or other "kitchen cleaners" since these can permanently mar your car's finish.

□ To dry your car, use a soft, worn terry towel or lint-free rag so you won't scratch your car's finish.

□ If you prefer to go to a professional car wash, choose one that uses rotating sponges or rubber strips rather than brushes. Try to find a car wash that will clean the inside as well as the outside of your car. (Recently car "detailing" has become popular. At these shops, for a hefty fee, professional car washers will spend hours washing and buffing your car to a clean-as-new sparkle, even using toothbrushes to work on insignias and tough-to-get-at areas. If you really care about your car's appearance, this extra service may be of interest to you, once a year or so.)

Car-waxing Tips

□ The wax on your car's surface serves not only to give it a glossy look, but also to protect the car's body from outside elements that can "eat away" its finish. Each time it rains, or every time you wash your car, take note of whether or not the water beads up into droplets atop your hood, roof, and trunk.

If it does, your car's wax is still working. If it doesn't, you need to wax again. In general, you should wax your car at least twice a year and more often if you drive in industrial city areas.

☐ Park outdoors away from direct sunlight, in a shaded area. (A hot car surface will cause wax to harden and dry too fast, making it more difficult to buff the car.)

☐ Apply the wax according to package directions. Have lots of dry, soft towels or rags on hand. Once the wax dries to a film on the car's surface, gently "buff" it off.

☐ Wax small sections of the car at a time—half the trunk, one fender, etc.—so the wax doesn't dry for too long, making it too difficult to buff off.

☐ Don't use wax on vinyl or plastic trim on cars as it can dull and damage these materials. Instead, "polish" a car's trim with a gentle silicone spray or an all-purpose cleaner whose label specifies that it's safe for vinyl and plastic surfaces.

Paint Touch-ups

☐ Shortly after you buy a car, ask your dealer for the number of the paint that matches your particular automobile, then buy a container of that paint to have on hand. Usually touch-up paint comes in nail-polish-sized containers with its own brush, and is easy to apply.

☐ Even the best-kept automobiles occasionally get nicks and tiny scratches and they're best taken care of right away—before rust and other corrosives set in. Clean off the areas around nicks on your car surface, and carefully "touch up" the spot with a little paint. Doing this as soon as you notice scratches can prevent the spread of rust, and the chipping away of more paint.

YOUR CHOICE OF FUEL

When it comes to fueling an automobile, there is no such thing as "pure" gasoline. The components of gasoline depend on its manufacturer and on the weather characteristics of the area in which it is going to be used, and your car. Different grades of gasoline are blended with different hydrocarbons and additives. Some gasolines contain anti-icing additives to prevent carburetor damage in cold weather; antirust additives and detergents in fuel can help to prevent corrosion and keep the fuel system clean; antioxidants and inhibitors prevent gummy fuel residue deposits in the carburetor and intake system.

Other additives increase a fuel's *octane rating*. High-octane ratings mean the fuel is able to be heated and compressed more before being ignited by a firing spark plug than low-octane fuels. In leaded gasolines, the higher the lead content, the higher the octane rating. In unleaded gasoline, other additives increase octane ratings.

You can see these octane ratings on the fuel pumps when you pull into your service station. Most leaded gasolines have an octane rating around 89. The octane rating of regular unleaded gasoline is around 87; and of premium unleaded gasolines, from 91 to 93.

Why is it important to know about differences in gasolines and octane ratings? Because the gasoline you put into your car can greatly affect its performance. Though high-octane gasoline is more expensive than lower grades, it can pay off in the long run if your engine needs the higher octane. Using a lower octane gasoline than your car requires can cause the air/fuel mixture to ignite before it should, meaning fuel is being burned inefficiently, leading to lower overall gas mileage, a "knock" or "ping" sound when you're driving, and generally poor engine performance.

On the other hand, not all engines require high-octane fuel and you're wasting money if you buy it needlessly. To determine what kind of fuel your car needs, check the manufacturer's recommendations in your owner's manual. If your car was manufactured from 1975 on, chances are it will require unleaded gas. That was the year most automakers chose to meet the Environmental Protection Agency's (EPA's) stiffer exhaust emission standards with a device called the catalytic converter. Engines fitted with catalytic converters must run on unleaded gas to avoid damaging the catalyst.

When to Use Higher Octane Fuel

Most cars today are manufactured to run on unleaded *regular* gasoline rather than premium brands. But through the life of your car, there may be times when you'll need to fill up with high-octane gas. Among them:

☐ If you begin to hear "pinging" or "knocking" when you're driving (progressively more likely as your car ages).

☐ If you have a malfunction in your car's emission system.

☐ If you're overdue for a tune-up and your car's timing is slightly off.

Driving to Conserve Fuel

☐ Never put leaded fuel in a car that specifically recommends unleaded fuel (as do most cars sold in the United States since 1975). It could greatly damage auto parts, particularly your catalytic converter.

☐ When possible, avoid start-and-stop driving, and try not to let your car idle for long periods of time.

☐ Minimize your use of car accessories—air conditioning is gas guzzling.

☐ Try to fill up your gas tank before it gets lower than 1/8 full; the gas at the bottom of your tank might contain sediment that has sunk to the bottom and could damage engine parts if it circulates.

☐ Even on cold mornings, it's better to drive off immediately than to let your car "warm up" for too long.

TIRES

The way you maintain your tires can affect not only the smoothness of your car's ride, but more subtle, important factors like fuel efficiency, the longevity of the tires, and most importantly, safety. Two drivers could buy identical sets of tires from the same dealer, but one set could last years longer than the other. Chances are this difference is not due to the construction of the tires, but to the way you maintain them.

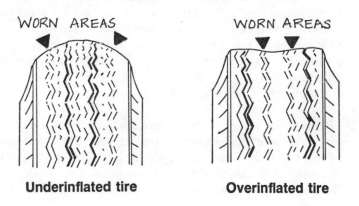

Underinflated tire   **Overinflated tire**

The most important factor in good tire care is proper inflation. *Overinflated tires* wear out unevenly and quickly in the center, and can cause a car to ride roughly. They are more prone to pick up nails or glass which could cause an air leak or blowout. *Underinflated tires* wear out more rapidly on the outside and can cut down on fuel economy. They can heat up more rapidly, leading to possible tire failure, and in general, cause "sloppy handling" by not gripping the road the way they should to allow for easy turns and stops—especially dangerous in wet weather. *(Hint:* if your tires "squeal" when you drive around corners, they could be underinflated.) For recommendations on how to handle a tire blowout, see pages 93–94.

You can't tell if a tire is improperly inflated just by looking at it—particularly if you have radial tires, which tend to look more squat or bulgy than other tire types. To check tire inflation, use a tire pressure gauge, available for under $10 at auto supply stores. Make this routine check monthly and always before any long drive.

How to Check Tire Pressure

Check for a sticker on the inside of the driver's doorjamb, on the door itself, or on the glove compartment door with instructions regarding correct air pressure for the tires on your car. The pressure will be in units of pounds per square inch (psi).

Always check tire pressure when tires are cold—when you've driven no more than three miles. A tire can heat up rapidly, and give you an erroneously high reading of air pressure if measured when warm. To measure tire pressure:

1)   Remove the valve cap on the tire, and in one swift motion, cover the valve with the circular part of your pressure gauge.
2)   Press the gauge down until you no longer hear the hiss of air coming out of the air valve. At this point, the "ruler" part of the gauge will spring out and indicate a certain number (for example, 30).
3)   If the gauge's number is the same as the number on your sticker, your tire is properly inflated.
4)   If the gauge's number is higher than the psi range, you may need to let out a little air by pressing down on the pin in the tire valve with your fingernail, pen, the protruding point on the other side of the pressure gauge, or other convenient object. Don't let out too much air before checking the pressure again. Keep checking until the gauge registers at the correct figure.
5)   If the tire gauge's number is lower than the psi range, you need to add air. To do this, remove the hose from the air pump

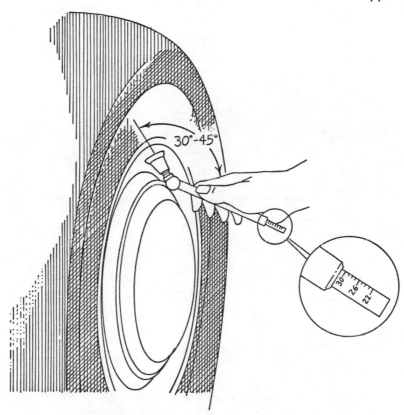

Checking tire pressure

at your service station, and turn the pump crank until the number on the pump is one or two numbers above your desired pressure. This compensates for differences in this gauge compared to your gauge. With the same rapid motion that you used to cover the valve with your tire gauge (as shown on the above illustration), cover the valve with the air hose. The pump should sound a few quick "dings"; when they stop, you should quickly remove the air hose from the valve. Use your tire pressure gauge to check the inflation again, and if your tires are now properly inflated, replace the valve cap. If

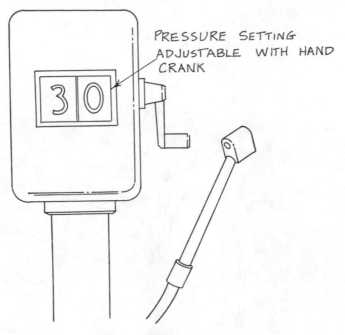

PRESSURE SETTING ADJUSTABLE WITH HAND CRANK

Station hose air pump

not, adjust the pressure until it measures correctly on your gauge. (It's important that all tire valves are covered by caps to keep out dirt and moisture.)

Your service station's air pump might be able to act as a pressure gauge if you don't have one, but try to go to a station as close to your home as possible so your tires don't heat up too much before you check their pressure. Just crank the air pump until the meter reads a number at the desired pressure. Let a little air out of your tires, then put the air hose over the valve and add air until the bell stops. If the air pump is working properly, it won't overinflate your tires, but will stop automatically when the pressure equals that on the meter. It's better, though, to rely on your own gauge to measure final pressure. Individual pump gauges at service stations are not known for great accuracy.

EXTRA TIPS:

☐ Always remember to check the inflation in your spare tire along with your other tires. If you have a special spare that is stored uninflated, check the aerosol pressure canister for damage regularly.

☐ If you're pulling a trailer, carrying an especially heavy load, or heading out on a very long highway drive, inflate your tires at the maximum pressure, if more than one is suggested on the label—but *never* over the maximum on the tire's sidewall.

☐ If any tire continually needs air, it probably has a leak and should be checked out, and, if necessary, repaired or replaced.

How to Check Tire Treads

Years ago, if you wanted to check your tire treads, you inserted a Lincoln penny into the treads head first; if the tread came up to Lincoln's forehead, your tires were still in good shape.

Today, manufacturers have enabled us to be more precise in measuring tire treads by installing "tread-wear bars" on most tires. These are narrow strips of smooth rubber that will show up at regular spots between rows of squiggly grooves on your

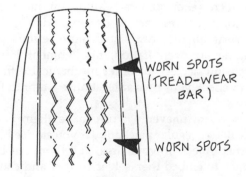

WORN SPOTS (TREAD-WEAR BAR)

WORN SPOTS

Worn tire

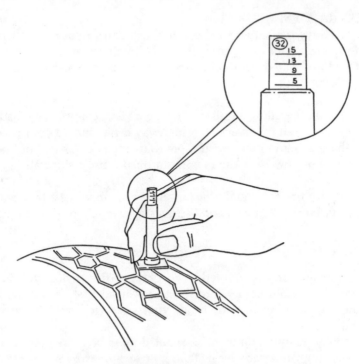

Tread-wear gauge in tire
(If ruler springs up to "2," it's time to get new tires.)

tires after they are worn down. You can also use a ruler or a tread-wear gauge to determine if the tread is worn down to 1/16 of an inch (expressed as 2/32nds on most tread-wear gauges); if so, your tires need to be replaced.

Uneven wear on tires can signal more serious problems—including under- or overinflation, misalignment, improper balance, suspension neglect, or other mechanical difficulties. It's important to check your tires at least once a month for signs of uneven wear.

If your tires are unevenly worn, have them inspected by your tire dealer or regular mechanic. If you notice bits of glass, metal or other objects in your tires, pull them out before they have a chance to embed themselves further and cause leaks or blowouts. If you notice lumps or bulges in a tire, this could mean that the internal layers of the tire have separated. Have your tires examined immediately by a professional.

Balance and Alignment

It's one of the first things you learn in any physics class: when an unbalanced wheel spins at a certain speed, there are specific spots on that wheel that are likely to hit the ground over and over again, because of vibrations induced by the force of gravity. The process of balancing your tires, then, is one of identifying the light spots on your tires as they spin. Then small weights are added to the edge of the wheel at those places to make sure that the force with which the tire hits the road is uniform.

Your tires should be balanced by the dealership when your car is new, and their balance should be checked yearly thereafter by a professional repair shop with suitable equipment. Today, many repair shops have sophisticated machines that precisely measure your tires' imbalance.

Unbalanced tires can make the car shake as you drive. Seat vibration suggests rear-wheel imbalance; steering wheel vibration indicates front-wheel imbalance. Unbalanced tires are more likely to wear out quickly in certain spots.

Have your regular repair shop check your wheel alignment, too. Misaligned wheels can cause hard steering, increased gas consumption, and quick, irregular tire wear. To check for misaligned tires: briefly let go of your steering wheel on a smooth, straight, level road. Does the car drift to the left or right side? If so, your tires might need to be realigned.

In checking alignment, your mechanic will be examining three aspects of your wheels: *camber, toe angle,* and *caster.* In checking wheel "camber," the mechanic makes sure that the wheels are aimed in such a way that the tires remain upright—don't lean outward or inward too much at the top (positive camber and negative camber, respectively).

The "toe angle" of your wheels refers to the direction your tires point when they're traveling down the road; they should point straight ahead, not "toe-in" ("pigeon-toed") or "toe-out" (like a penguin).

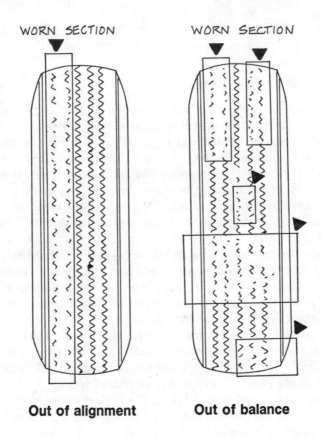

WORN SECTION

WORN SECTION

Out of alignment

Out of balance

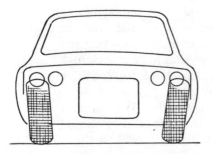

Positive camber

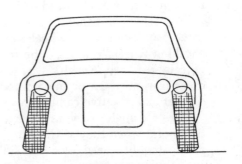

Negative camber

FRONT OF CAR

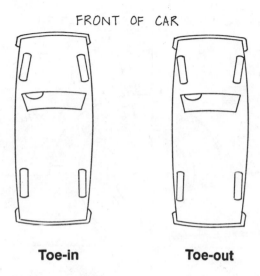

Toe-in   **Toe-out**

To understand "caster," think of furniture casters. Looking at the way a caster is set on a chair leg, for example, you'll probably notice that the chair leg is not over the center of the wheel. When the chair is pushed in any direction, the castered wheel pivots so that the wheel's contact point with the floor always trails behind the pivot axis of the caster in the chair leg. In this manner, an unrestrained, castered wheel always seeks the position of greatest directional stability. A car's designers determine the optimum caster setting ("positive caster angle") or offset of the front wheels' steering axes to give the car good directional stability in straight-ahead driving. When the caster is off due to misalignment, your car will be difficult to drive in a straight line. Think of how difficult it is to steer a shopping cart when the front wheels insist on leading on their pivot axes, instead of trailing smoothly along behind them.

Driving over a deep pothole or a bad bump can cause a wheel rim to bend, or damage the body of a tire (sometimes with no apparent outer damage to the tire). Such poor road conditions can decrease fuel efficiency, and cause more repairs to tires and other parts of your car. So it's up to you, as a driver, to try to avoid rough spots in the road. Keep attuned to

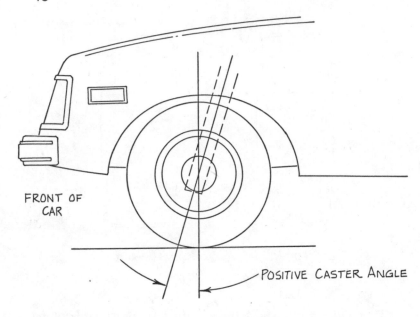

FRONT OF
CAR

POSITIVE CASTER ANGLE

wheel alignment, especially if you frequently drive over rough roads, and have a professional alignment check once a year.

Driving Habits That Prolong Tire Life

Good driving habits can ensure that your tires receive a clean bill of health each time you or a professional examines them. Here are some suggestions:

☐ Avoid fast starts, stops, and turns.

☐ Never "peel" (accelerate extremely fast so that the tires spin).

☐ Whenever possible, avoid potholes, bumps, and objects in the road.

☐ Don't drive up on curbs or let the tires' sidewalls scrape against a curb when parking.

☐ Have your tires rotated as often as suggested in your owner's manual or at least every year, to make sure tires wear out evenly. Rotation is especially important if you have a front-wheel drive car. In such cars, the front wheels do a greater percentage of steering, propelling, and braking work than in a rear-drive car. This makes the front tires wear quicker. The latest advice for tires, including radials, calls for a criss-cross, back-to-front rotation pattern: right front to left rear, left rear to left front, left front to right rear, right rear to right front.

☐ Never leave snow tires on beyond the snow season, as they will wear out too quickly.

☐ After any repair work on your tires, make sure the tires' nuts (see illustration, p. 100) are securely replaced. Sometimes mechanics do not turn them as hard as they should and they can ease off while you're driving, causing the wheel itself to loosen. Also, make sure that the valve caps are securely replaced to keep out dirt and contaminants.

OIL

Technically, of course, engine oil could never be labeled a car "part"; but go without oil and you might as well try driving without an engine. Your car's oil keeps all its parts in working order. Oil helps monitor your auto's temperatures by flowing from the hot spots in the engine through the parts of your car's cooling system. It acts as a cushion between engine parts so they don't rub against each other, causing parts to overheat and wear rapidly. Engine oil has to be thin enough to flow smoothly through your car's system, yet thick enough to coat engine parts sufficiently, and the hotter your engine gets, the thicker your oil should be. That's why a change in seasons might warrant a change in oil viscosity (or "thickness"). Today's compact engines hold less oil than the larger engine gas guzzlers—all the more reason to choose a high quality oil, to keep track of your car's oil level and condition, and to change your oil on a regular basis.

What Kind of Oil Should You Buy?

With all the heavy demands that today's complex engine puts on oil, you will want to know what is the correct type of oil for your car. The easiest way to find out is to consult your owner's manual and make sure that your mechanic or anyone who changes your oil does the same. All cars should use the highest quality oil for the most protection against wear. This oil is identified by the American Petroleum Institute (API) as API–SF.

Oil viscosity is indicated by a number or numbers on the container ranging from 5–50. It is not a measure of overall oil quality. The higher the number, the thicker the oil. You should use lower-numbered oil in cold weather; higher-numbered oil in hot climates; or a multi-viscosity oil indicated by a range of numbers—10W–30, for example—for variable climates. (The "W" means that the number preceding it is the low temperature viscosity rating, which is important for winter use.) All engine oil containers have the letters SAE with the viscosity numbers (e.g., SAE 10W–30); they stand for "Society of Automotive Engineers" and they indicate that the oil meets the viscosity requirements set by this group.

Multi-viscosity oils have become increasingly popular with car owners as the oils can alter their thickness to meet the challenges of changing outdoor temperatures and different driving conditions. However, if you live in an area whose climate is pretty stable—Southern California or Florida, for example—a single-grade oil might be all your car needs. It's a good idea to consult your owner's manual and your dealer for the correct oil viscosity to use for the temperatures expected between now and the next oil change.

One tip: once you've decided on a particular engine oil, it's best (but not imperative) to stick with that brand whenever you need to add oil. Different brands have different chemical additives and there's no guarantee that any *two* brands are going to be completely compatible. Major problems, though, are very rare.

How to Check Your Oil

While it's a good idea to be alert to the warning signs on your dashboard, waiting for the "Oil" light to flash on is *not* an adequate way to keep track of your car's oil level. By the time the warning light goes on—and by the time you notice it— engine parts have been running dry at least for a few seconds, and that's long enough to cause significant damage.

When your car has used up only one quart of oil, it's time to replenish your oil supply. (Most cars today hold about three to five quarts of oil.) Check your oil level every time you buy gas or take any long drive. It's very simple to do, and convenient as well, due to self-service stations that are becoming ever more popular across the country.

1) First, make sure your car is parked on level ground. Parking on a slope may alter the reading one way or another. Turn off your engine; if your engine is running, you will not get an accurate reading.
2) Look under your car's hood for the oil dipstick. You can spot it by its metal ring popping up from the maze of tubes and wires. The ring is brightly colored on some new cars for quicker identification.
3) Pull out the dipstick and wipe it clean using a lint-free rag.
4) Push the dipstick back into its tube all the way down; a few seconds later, pull it out and lay it horizontally in the palm of your other hand. If the line that indicates "quart down" or "add" is clearly visible, uncovered by oil, you need to add a quart. *(See illustration,* page 22.)

How to Add Oil

These days, many engine oils come in plastic quart-sized bottles with narrow spouts that are much easier to use than the metal oil cans that had to be opened with a can opener. Still, it's important to be careful not to spill oil on the outside of the engine, as splattered oil can collect dirt. Also, most plastic containers are sealed with foil under the cap; be sure none of the foil gets into the engine and down in the oil.

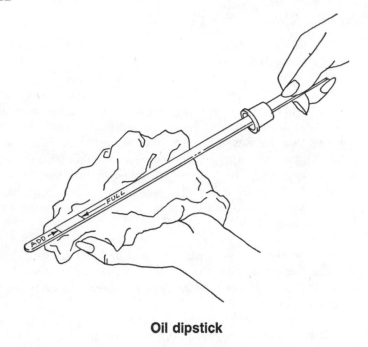

Oil dipstick

1) When you add oil, your engine should be turned off and the oil cap should be cool enough so you don't burn your hand.

2) Using a rag to protect your hand, unscrew the oil cap and carefully begin pouring the oil into the oil-fill hole.

3) Once the quart container of oil is empty, wait a few minutes for the oil to run to the bottom of the engine.

4) Check the oil level again by pulling the dipstick out of the oil-fill hole. It should be just below "full." Never overfill the engine with oil as this could cause oil to be churned up too much in the engine, lessening the oil's lubricating ability.

When you're breaking in a new car, it's especially important to check oil frequently as engine parts wearing into one another create excessive heat, and new engines use more oil than

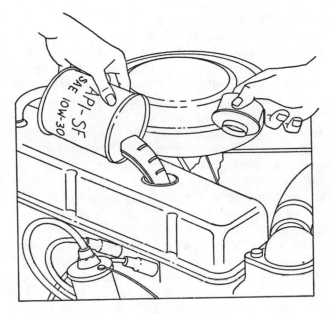

Adding oil

a slightly older car. Very old cars also use more oil, because parts that don't seal as efficiently as when new increase the oil that is burned inside the engine. In brand new or very old cars, you may have to add oil as frequently as once a month.

If your car is well broken in but not old, however, having to add oil more than once a month may signal other problems:

—you may have an oil leak. To check for oil leaks, spread a newspaper underneath your parked car overnight. Next morning, see if there are any oil drips on the paper. (If any nonoil drips are on the paper, your car may be leaking coolant, windshield washer fluid, transmission fluid, or something else. See pages 88–89 for more information.)

—if you don't have an oil leak, your oil may be the wrong viscosity and you may need thicker oil with a higher SAE number.

—your valve-stem seals or piston rings inside the engine could be allowing oil into places it shouldn't be. Such internal "leaks" could require a major repair to solve the problem. Look over all the parts under your hood to see if there seems to be any excess oil on the outside of them. If so—or if you still can't determine what's wrong—have your mechanic look at your car.

During an oil change, the mechanic will put your car up on a lift, place a big collection can underneath your engine, remove your oil filter, then the drain plug, causing a steady flow of oil to pour out into the can. (Though an oil change is easy enough for any car owner to do, it's extremely messy. Unless you *own* a lift and all the proper tools, you'll probably prefer to have your oil changed by a professional.) While the oil is draining, the mechanic will often give a car a "lube job" if it needs one; many newer cars never do. In a lube job, the mechanic greases the fittings in all the steering and differential components. Once all the old oil has drained out, the mechanic will install a new oil filter, and replace the drain plug. Then he'll add the proper number of quarts of oil into the opening in the engine's crankcase. While your car is up on the lift, your mechanic may give its underside a quick look-over, including checking the muffler, catalytic converter, and exhaust pipe for loose connections, rust, or leaks; and checking the chassis for bent, cracked, or loose components.

If you hear rattling when driving your car out of the shop after an oil change, it just means that your oil is circulating through the engine. This noise should stop after a few seconds. Be sure to check your oil soon after an oil change; *a rapid loss of oil could mean that the mechanic has forgotten to replace the drain plug.*

When to Change Your Oil

Throughout the life of your car, parts are constantly wearing into one another and as they do so, microscopic filings may be etched off parts and picked up by the oil. Such wearing-in is especially heavy during the "break-in" period of a new car (see page 159). These filings, plus dirt from the road and air, can enter the engine, causing parts to wear more quickly and work less efficiently. For this reason, it's necessary, periodically, to drain your car of its old "dirty" oil and replace it with fresh "healthy" oil.

Your car owner's manual will give you general directions for when to change your oil, if you drive under "ideal" conditions. But everyone knows that it's impossible to drive only under "ideal" weather, road, or traffic conditions. Most owner's manuals will recommend an oil change every 6,000 miles or so; but dedicated car buffs say to increase the frequency to every 3,000 miles to ensure that your car will run smoother longer. You can never change the oil too frequently, but you can do great damage to your car if you don't change it often enough.

REASONS TO CHANGE YOUR OIL MORE FREQUENTLY:

Certain conditions may make your oil get dirty faster than under "ideal" driving conditions, and you should be especially careful to check your oil—and to have it changed, when necessary—in the following instances:

☐ If you use your car often in stop-start city driving, especially in cold weather.

☐ If you use your car to haul trailers or any heavy loads, since hard-working engines tend to build up more heat in very high temperatures.

☐ If you drive often on very dusty roads. (These conditions also warrant that you pay special attention to all your car's filters.)

☐ If you use your car for prolonged high-speed driving. (This is one reason why it's important to check, and perhaps change, your oil before a long trip.)

☐ If you have a very new or a very old car.

RADIATOR

Your radiator is the heart of your car's cooling system *(see illustration,* page 57). Inside your engine the temperature can rise to as high as 5,000° F. Coolant—a mixture of chemicals and water—absorbs the heat from the engine, and through a system of fans and hoses, cools it down before reentering the radiator. When all goes well, this process prevents the engine from overheating.

In the event that your engine *does* overheat, you should never remove the pressure cap (located at the top of your radiator) to check coolant level until you first allow the engine to cool down. The hot fluid under pressure in the radiator could spurt out of an open cap, scalding you if it contacts your skin. (For what to do if your car overheats, see page 119.)

On most cars the antifreeze should be flushed out and replaced with fresh coolant every other year. Antifreeze coolant is an ethylene-glycol chemical that has additives to prevent

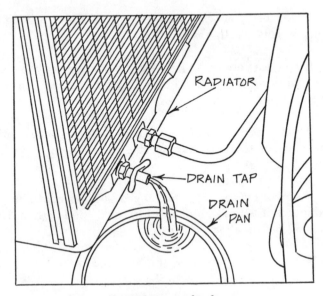

Draining coolant

accumulation of rust, corrosion, and scale throughout your auto's systems, and after two years, these additives lose their effectiveness. The aluminum radiators in some new autos can corrode more readily than older radiators, and rust and corroded products can clog the radiators, causing the engine to overheat.

How to Change Radiator Coolant (Antifreeze)

You can change the radiator coolant yourself, but if you suspect there's severe corrosion in your radiator system, have it done professionally. Here are the basic steps to drain the old coolant from your car's system:

1) Use pliers to open the "petcock" drain (a little "faucet" found at the bottom of the radiator) or disconnect the lower radiator hose (if your radiator doesn't have a petcock), and allow the old coolant to drain out completely into a collection bin. *(See illustration,* facing page.)
2) Pour a cooling system cleaner (available at auto supply stores) into the radiator to flush out the system, following the directions on the container.
3) Replace the petcock, or radiator hose, and add a 50/50 proportion of antifreeze and water directly into your radiator.
4) Replace the radiator pressure cap; then start the engine and let it idle for a few minutes so the system can warm up and the coolant can circulate.
5) Stop the engine and let it cool for a few minutes; then remove the radiator pressure cap and fill the radiator to the top with coolant. Fill the coolant recovery reservoir *(see illus.,* p. 28) with antifreeze/water mixture (with the aid of a siphon, if practical). Check the coolant level the next time you drive the car to see if it needs replenishing or "topping off."

How to Check Your Radiator Thermostat

The thermostat controls your automobile's cooling system by sensing changes in coolant temperature and regulating the flow of coolant in order to maintain the most efficient operat-

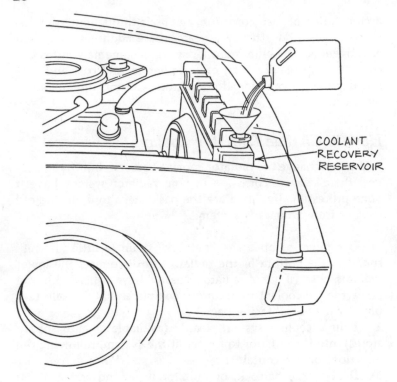

COOLANT
RECOVERY
RESERVOIR

Adding coolant

ing temperature. This, in turn, increases fuel efficiency and reduces engine wear.

Thermostats *do* fail and when this happens, it creates a situation in which your engine could easily overheat. However, you can easily prevent this problem by keeping tabs on the condition of your thermostat with this simple check:

1) With your transmission in "park" and the parking brake applied, start the engine and let it run at normal idle speed for up to ten minutes.

2) Grasp the upper radiator hose, while the engine is idling. If the engine is cool, the thermostat is closed, hence, very little

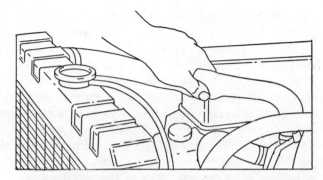

**Feeling the temperature of the top radiator
hose to check that the thermostat is open**

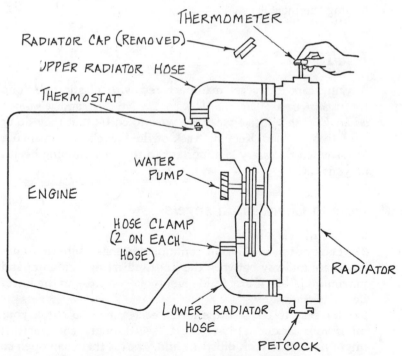

THERMOMETER

RADIATOR CAP (REMOVED)

UPPER RADIATOR HOSE

THERMOSTAT

WATER
PUMP

ENGINE

HOSE CLAMP
(2 ON EACH
HOSE)

RADIATOR

LOWER RADIATOR
HOSE

PETCOCK

190° F. thermometer in the radiator

coolant will be flowing from the engine through the upper hose. When the engine begins to heat up during idle, the thermostat should open and you should be able to feel the warm coolant flowing through the hose. *(See illus.,* p. 29.)

3) If you suspect that your thermostat is not opening and closing correctly (e.g., if you *don't* feel a warm surge of coolant through the hose as the engine heats up), place a metal kitchen or candy thermometer into the radiator filler neck while the engine is cold. *(See illus.,* p. 29.) Start the engine and let it idle as before. When the coolant begins to flow, and the thermostat opens to allow the coolant to flow, the thermometer should read about 190° F. for most cars. If the temperature does not rise near this point, your thermostat most likely needs to be replaced. (The thermostat is an inexpensive component to replace—especially compared to the costs of damaged engine parts caused by overheating because of a neglected malfunctioning thermostat.)

FLUID LEVELS

Many cars today are manufactured with plastic reservoirs for *radiator coolant, brake fluid, power steering fluid,* and *windshield washer fluid,* and once a week it's wise to check that they don't need to be refilled. Keeping track of fluid levels, and changing fluids when necessary is important to the long-running health of your car.

How to Check Fluid Levels

1) Lift the car's hood.

2) Look at the translucent containers to make sure that fluid levels are midway between the lines indicating minimum and maximum levels. If any fluid level looks too close to the lower line, add fluid.

3) It's easy to check these levels each time you check your oil. If your car doesn't have these "see-through" containers, it might have ones with dipsticks and/or caps that snap open so

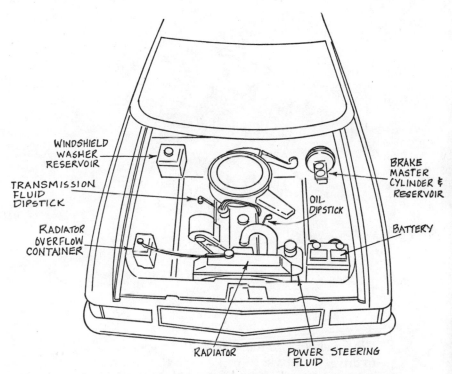

WINDSHIELD WASHER RESERVOIR

TRANSMISSION FLUID DIPSTICK

RADIATOR OVERFLOW CONTAINER

BRAKE MASTER CYLINDER & RESERVOIR

OIL DIPSTICK

BATTERY

RADIATOR

POWER STEERING FLUID

Typical locations of fluid levels to be checked

you can peer inside (see page 32). Just follow your owner's manual instructions.

How to Check Transmission Fluid

Automatic transmission fluid should be checked once a month. Following is a general explanation of how to do it. You should compare this procedure to the one outlined in your owner's manual; follow your owner's manual guidelines if they differ greatly from those below.

1) Park your car on level ground, start the engine, and let it

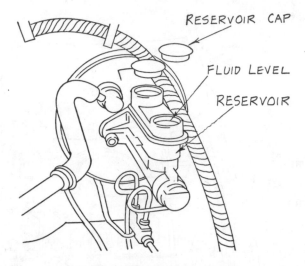

Reservoir for brake fluid

idle for about two minutes. With your parking brake on, shift to drive, then back to park.

2) While the engine is still running, gently pull out the dipstick located close to the back of the hood, near the firewall. *(See illustration,* page 31.) Be sure that you are not removing the engine oil dipstick.

3) Carefully touch the wet end of the dipstick to make sure the fluid is warm (necessary for an accurate reading). If it feels cold, replace the dipstick and drive your car around the neighborhood for five minutes or so.

4) If the fluid is warm, clean the dipstick with a lint-free rag, and push it back until the cap seats on the rim. A few seconds later, pull the dipstick out and lay it horizontally in the palm of your other hand, as you would to check your oil (see page 22).

5) If the fluid is between the two notches on the dipstick, there's no need to add fluid. If it's very close to the bottom notch, add a pint, not a quart. You will need a long funnel to add the fluid to the same tube that holds the transmission's dipstick.

6) The transmission fluid should be deep red in color; if it's brownish, it's probably getting old and should be changed soon.

FILTERS

Keeping track of fluid levels, and changing fluids when necessary, is important to the long-running health of your car. But you're defeating your good intentions if you don't check and change the filters through which those fluids pass as well. For example, if your mechanic changes your oil, but leaves in your old oil filter, you're passing the fresh oil through a dirty filter and the oil is not going to stay clean for long.

Most cars have six filters that need to be changed periodically. The first four are: the *crankcase vent filter,* which prevents dirt from entering the crankcase; the *air filter,* under the big circular lid in the middle of your engine, which keeps dirt, dust, bugs, leaves, and other abrasive objects out of your carburetor's air intake; the *fuel filter,* which traps rust, sediment, dirt, and other substances that could clog the tiny jets of your carburetor; and the *vapor canister filter,* which cleans the air entering the engine through the evaporative emission control system.

Underneath your car are two other filters—the *oil filter* on the engine, which traps dirt, metal filings, and sludge so only clean, filtered oil can circulate through your engine; and the *automatic transmission filter,* which traps similar particles in that precision part of your car.

Generally your mechanic should replace your oil filter every time he changes your oil (which, ideally, would be every 3,000 miles or so). Your transmission filter and vapor canister filter should probably be replaced every two years or 24,000 miles; your air filter and crankcase vent, every one to two years or 12,000–24,000 miles; and your fuel filter, every year or 12,000 miles.

In most cars, the only filter that you can actually examine before you change it is your air filter.

How to Check Your Air Filter

1) Unscrew the metal lid that covers the air filter.
2) Hold the filter up to a bare light bulb. If you can see light through its tiny holes clearly, it's probably still in good shape. If you can't see any light through the tiny filter holes, you need to replace the filter. If the filter is very dirty, it can restrict air entering the engine, causing your car to burn extra gasoline needlessly, a situation that could cost you much more money in the long run than the $10 or so that a new air filter costs.

HOSES AND BELTS

Every time you raise your hood to check your oil, you should give everything underneath a quick "once-over." By making such a cursory examination a habit, you'll get to know what's "normal" for your engine and be alert to the earliest signs of trouble. In addition to this quick observation, you should examine your hoses and belts at least once a month.

Such routine checkups can be especially helpful when it comes to knowing what's proper for your car's belts and hoses. Replace any worn, loose, or bulging hoses or rusted, worn clamps immediately. Also replace any frayed, loose, or slick-looking belts. Usually if one belt or hose needs to be replaced, the others are probably in poor shape, too. Since belts often overlap other belts and hoses overlap other hoses (see p. 38), the mechanic often has to remove one belt to get to the other, so you might as well have them all changed at once.

Once your mechanic has replaced a hose, check to make sure it's not touching any moving or hot engine parts. If a replaced belt or hose is still whole, ask to have it back and put it in your trunk. In an on-the-road emergency, such spare hoses and belts could temporarily replace a blown hose or snapped belt long enough to get you to a service station without having to be towed. It's also a good idea to carry extra hose clamps in

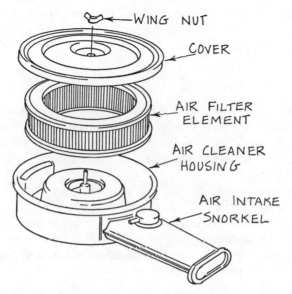

WING NUT

COVER

AIR FILTER ELEMENT

AIR CLEANER HOUSING

AIR INTAKE SNORKEL

Parts of an air filter

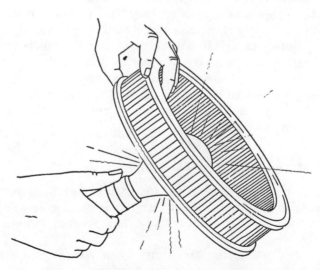

Using a light to check the air filter

your trunk to reinstall a popped-off hose, and heavy-duty tape to seal small hose leaks long enough to get you to a service station to replace the hose.

How to Check Belts

1) Look under your hood, when your engine is turned off and cool. You'll see belts connected to different components of your car, including the engine-cooling fan, the water and power steering pumps, the alternator, and the air conditioner, if you have one.

2) Gently press each belt midway between its pulleys to check its tension. If you've been checking the belts since your car was new, you'll know what feels normal in terms of tension. Usually, when pressed, a belt should deflect no more than half an inch. Too little tension can cause a belt to slip and fail to operate the various components it drives; too much tension could cause the belt to wear out too quickly and stretch, or snap off altogether.

3) If you suspect your belts are worn, but you're not sure, a mechanic can test them with a belt-tension gauge.

4) Check to see if belts are frayed along the edges or have a slick, shiny appearance. If so, they have probably worn down to a dangerously thin point and should be replaced. The average lifespan of a belt is four years, but it's much better to replace them when you first notice that they're worn than waiting for one to snap when you're on the highway, miles from your service station. A loose or slipping belt can cause overheating, a dead battery, a loss of power steering assist, or inefficient air conditioning.

How to Check Hoses

It is important to exercise care when you examine your car's hoses. Flexible rubber hoses carry fluids or gases from one engine component to another and over time, they can wear out.

1) Look under your car's hood when your engine is turned off and cool.

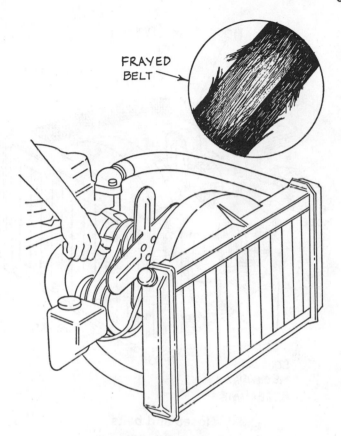

FRAYED BELT

Checking belt tension

2) Examine hoses carefully for cracks, leaks, and bulges, which usually appear first around the clamps where the hose is connected to its main component, such as the radiator, power steering mechanism, or transmission.

3) Examine the metal clamps that seal the hoses on their respective components' tubes for corrosion, and have a mechanic replace them if they look rusty or easy to snap. (A clamp that snaps off can set off an unfortunate chain of events: a hose could become unconnected, causing the fluid inside to leak

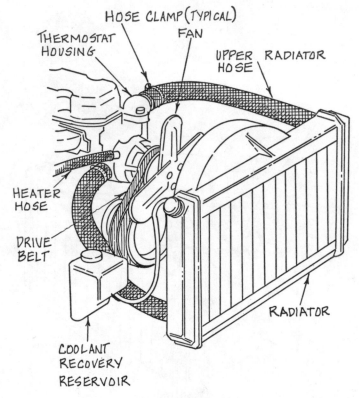

HOSE CLAMP (TYPICAL)

THERMOSTAT
HOUSING

FAN

UPPER RADIATOR
HOSE

HEATER
HOSE

DRIVE
BELT

RADIATOR

COOLANT
RECOVERY
RESERVOIR

Hoses and belts

out; this could cause damage to the engine and cause it to overheat.)

BATTERY

Batteries are part of your car's electrical system *(see illustration, page 52)* and function as the storage spot for the electricity on which your alternator depends. Today, many cars are manufactured with "maintenance-free" batteries, which are generally better able to handle sudden drops in outdoor temperatures than the batteries in cars made years ago. For maintenance-free batteries, you never need to (and usually cannot) check the battery fluid level since it remains constant. Some maintenance-free batteries do have a color indicator that tells you if the electrolyte—the mixture of acid añd water stored in a battery—is low. Like all batteries, even maintenance-free batteries can become corroded around the clamps. In non-maintenance-free batteries, you should check the fluid level at least once a month (weekly in hot weather).

How to Check the Battery

1) Unsnap the plastic caps on the battery's top and add water when necessary with a rubber bulb, in a non-maintenance-free battery.

2) Check the battery's clamps for corrosion. If they are corroded, they will not take a proper charge either from your alternator or from another car battery through jumper cables.

3) To neutralize corrosion and enable your battery to accept a

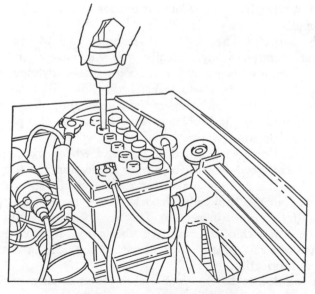

Adding water to a battery

charge, brush a mixture of equal parts water and baking soda over the clamps. After the clamps are dry, cover the tops of the clamps and their terminals with petroleum jelly to protect them from further corrosion.

4) Make sure that the battery cables are not worn and are securely connected.

5) Never smoke or light a match near a battery, because a battery normally gives off explosive hydrogen gas when charged. Also, since battery electrolyte is an acid solution, be especially cautious not to get any on your skin or clothing. Wash your hands immediately after touching any part of any auto battery.

BRAKES

Your brakes should be inspected once a year by a certified brake technician, and the brake fluid level in your master cylinder should be examined every 5,000 miles. Because a brake inspection involves removing the tires and checking components not usually visible from the outside, this is a job only for automotive professionals.

The inspection checklist should include: the fluid level in the master cylinder (though, ideally, you will have examined it weekly); brake lines that run from the master cylinder to all four wheels, for rust and leaks; brake hoses that run from brake lines to the brake calipers and wheel cylinders, for cracks or brittleness of the rubber seals; brake linings and pads, for excessive or uneven wear, glazing, or contamination from brake fluid or grease; brake calipers and wheel cylinders, for leaks; bearings and seals, for proper lubrication and temperature; and the parking brake, for any necessary adjustments. Often, your mechanic will "repack" your wheel bearings during a routine brake inspection. This involves cleaning the two bearings on each of the nondrive wheels (e.g., front wheels on a rear-drive car), putting fresh grease in each bearing to ensure proper lubrication.

In addition to having your brakes professionally examined regularly, you should keep attuned to brake performance every time you drive. Small abnormalities in brake response could indicate major problems that should be attended to immediately. (See page 72 for an illustration of the brake system and pages 91–92 for warning signs and diagnoses of brake problems.)

EXHAUST SYSTEM

About once every month, it's a good idea to check your car's exhaust components.

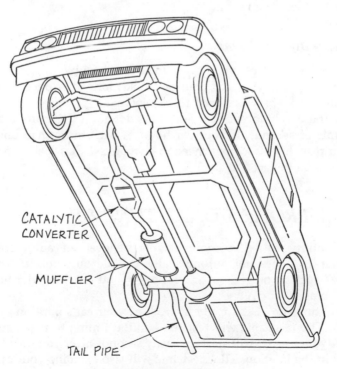

CATALYTIC
CONVERTER

MUFFLER

TAIL PIPE

Exhaust system

How to Check the Exhaust System

1)   Kneel behind your car and check your car's tailpipe. Shake it gently to make sure it's firmly connected to the muffler and is free from cracks, rust, and leaks.

2)   Check the muffler to see that it's secure and not rusted.

3)   Have your mechanic check the catalytic converter at least once a year; in most cases it won't wear out as fast as other exhaust system components, because most catalytic converters are made of higher alloy metals than other components.

SHOCK ABSORBERS AND SPRINGS

Your car's shock absorbers should be checked at least once a month. (See illustration, page 64.)

Checking for Wear

1)   Press down on your car's hood for a couple of seconds; then let go. If your car bounces back more than once, your front shock absorbers need to be replaced.

2)   Stand behind your car and press down on the trunk for a couple of seconds. If your car bounces back more than once, your rear shock absorbers need to be replaced. Shock absorbers should be replaced in pairs.

THE PROFESSIONAL TUNE-UP

Contrary to what some drivers believe, an automobile "tune-up" does not automatically include automobile "service" such as oil change and lube job, and checking the tires and brakes.

A "tune-up" is basically a check of your car's ignition system. The mechanic will test the ignition timing to make sure that your engine will start up easily seconds after you turn the key in the ignition. The mechanic will also examine your car's ignition wires and distributor components for wear; replace any worn spark plugs; check the PCV (Positive Crankcase Ventilation) valve for leaks; check the automatic choke to ensure it won't stick; and examine the distributor, rotor, and carburetor for adequate performance, making adjustments where necessary.

Tune-ups are conducted for one of two reasons: to maintain an engine that's running well, or to restore power to a poorly running engine. Before electronic ignitions came into being in the mid-1970s, it was easy to tell when your car needed a tune-up: it was hard to start (especially on cold mornings); it would idle roughly and sometimes make popping and metallic noises. Those were the days of "point" ignition systems, which worked by sending electricity through metal contacts in the distributor that opened and closed as they rubbed against other parts. Eventually, this rubbing contact made these parts wear out and they had to be replaced—usually several times during the average life of the automobile.

Today, computers have taken the place of points, and within your distributor, parts don't touch, so they don't wear away as quickly (if at all) as they used to. Generally today's electronic ignitions work much more precisely than the old point systems and last much longer. However, if they do become faulty, often your car will give you no warning—it just won't start one day. If they need repairs, today's more sophisticated systems can be very expensive to fix.

To stop trouble before it happens, have your car tuned up once a year, or every 12,000 miles, whichever comes first. Many dealerships and service stations have a sign hanging outside their door stating exactly what their tune-up service includes. If not, make sure to ask your mechanic. You shouldn't have to pay for a brake inspection if your brakes were already thoroughly inspected just a month ago. Conversely, if it's time for an oil change and for your tires and brakes to be checked, you should ask for those services specifically rather than assuming they'll be done.

For special tune-up servicing you may need before winter, see pages 123–24.

PROLONGING CAR LIFE

In this era of multi-car families, there's often a "second" car that's used primarily for quick trips and errands close to home. Frequent starts and stops when driving short distances can take their toll on your engine's parts. Those short drives don't allow your engine to warm up completely before it starts to cool off. These constantly changing operating temperatures cause excessive and rapid wear on car parts, particularly new parts that are still wearing into one another.

To prevent this unnecessary wear, take your car out on the highway every two weeks or so, and drive at the full speed limit for about a half hour—to get your car's "juices flowing." This will help car parts wear into each other evenly, and prevent oil and other fluids from sitting cold for too long, collecting sediments and sludge, and other potentially damaging particles.

STATE INSPECTIONS

Some states encourage drivers to maintain their automobiles by enforcing laws requiring mandatory state inspections. While from the state's point of view, the inspections are conducted to ensure that a vehicle is *safe* to drive, such inspections can also provide the added benefit of spotting a problem early, hence, prolonging car life. Check with your local motor vehicle department to see if your state has a periodic motor-vehicle inspection (PMVI) law. Laws vary from requiring only trucks or school buses to be inspected to requiring all vehicles to be thoroughly inspected twice a year (e.g., in New Hampshire).

In states that have such laws, you take your car to a mechanic certified to make such inspections, and if your car passes inspection, you're given a sticker to display on the corner of your windshield. If you fail to have your car inspected, you'll receive a hefty fine. Some automobile parts that are inspected under these laws include: the exhaust system, headlights, tires, horn, mirrors, windshield wipers, brakes, turn signals, and fuel system. Some regions have set up stringent limits for carbon monoxide and hydrocarbon exhaust emissions in certain municipalities to meet air quality requirements of the EPA. In these areas, inspectors have the additional responsibility of ensuring that auto emissions meet these standards.

2
A Layman's Guide
to How Your Car Operates

From reading the first chapter of this book, you should have a good idea of how to keep your automobile in top running condition. Now it's time to learn in more detail how a car actually works.

The average car today is a wonderful, complex machine comprised of some 15,000 parts, approximately 5,000 of which move during operation. Most of these parts are interdependent, which means if one little thing goes wrong it can set off a chain reaction that could interfere with the smooth-running performance of your entire car. Understanding how your car works and how different parts interact with one another will give you a better chance to understand why something goes wrong and what you can do to fix it.

Your car can be broken down into twelve interdependent "systems": the engine; the electrical system; the fuel system; the exhaust system; the cooling system; the lubricating system; the transmission; the driveshaft, differential, and rear and front axles; the steering system; the suspension system; tires; and brakes.

While each of these systems operates on its own, each also requires the interaction of other systems to work; and your car requires the use of *all* these systems to operate. In this chapter, you'll find basic explanations of how each main component of your car works, with references to where else in this book you can learn more about a particular part—such as what can go wrong and why, and what you might be able to do to solve a problem. In describing the way any machine operates, it's usual to start with the center of activity; in your car, this is the engine.

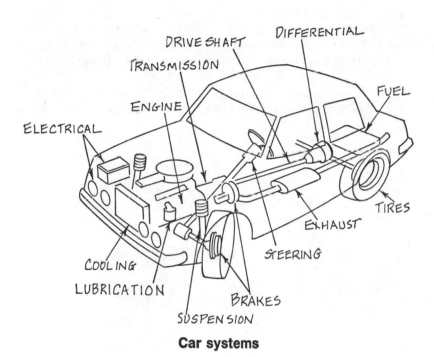

Car systems

THE ENGINE

For some drivers, the phenomenon of turning an ignition key and putting life into an immobile object is about as elusive and mysterious an idea as the reasons for the daily dawns and sunsets. You don't question it; you just accept it.

In fact, anyone who's able to drive a car should be able to understand the basic principle on which it operates; and it's worth understanding. The automobile runs on an internal combustion engine that gives your car the power it needs to move. Inside your engine, fuel and air mix and, via an electrical spark, are ignited and burn (or "combust"), thus creating thermal energy.

Your engine then undergoes a "four-stroke" process of turning this thermal energy into mechanical energy. This entails four events, which occur in split seconds within the *cylinders* in your engine. (The number of cylinders your engine has depends on the make of your car. Usually, the more cylinders, the more powerful the engine. Typical engines have four or six cylinders, and high-powered engines have eight. Today even a three-cylinder car has been developed.)

At the top of each cylinder are three holes, one of which is covered by a spark plug whose electrodes reach down into the

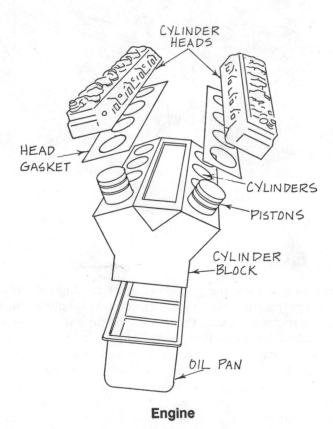

Engine

hollow chamber inside the cylinder. The other two holes are covered by valves somewhat similar to those on a trumpet. These valves open and close, in time with the action of the *pistons* below them. One is an "intake" valve; the other is an "exhaust" valve. When you turn your ignition key, you set off a chain of events to allow a proper mixture of air and fuel into your carburetor which, in turn, sends this mixture down to your engine. (In fuel-injected engines, the air and gas are squirted directly into the engine without the use of a carburetor.) Once the air/fuel mixture reaches the engine cylinder, four strokes set your engine in motion:

Stroke one—The "Induction Stroke": The cylinder intake valve opens, creating a vacuum inside the cylinder; the piston moves down pulling air and fuel with it, into the cylinder chamber.

Stroke two—The "Compression Stroke": Both cylinder valves close. The piston moves up, compressing the air/fuel mixture toward the top of the cylinder chamber, until the piston can go no further.

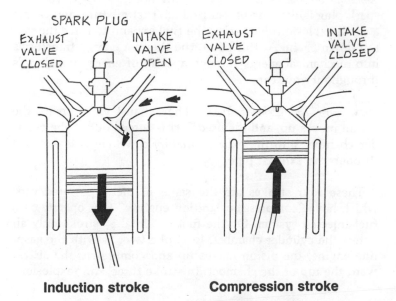

Induction stroke   **Compression stroke**

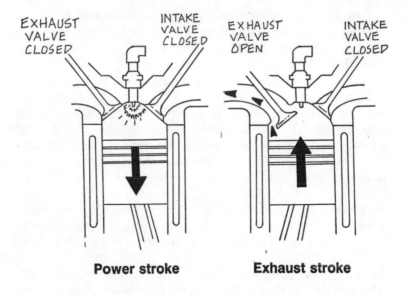

EXHAUST VALVE CLOSED

INTAKE VALVE CLOSED

EXHAUST VALVE OPEN

INTAKE VALVE CLOSED

Power stroke

Exhaust stroke

Stroke three—The "Power Stroke": With both valves closed, the spark plug ignites the pressurized air/fuel mixture, and causes a small explosion that makes the fuel expand to force the piston down again. At this point, the thermal energy transforms into mechanical energy through a series of energy transferrals throughout your car.

Stroke four—The "Exhaust Stroke": The exhaust valve opens, the piston moves up, and the used fuel is forced out of the cylinder chamber into the exhaust manifold, where it is expelled through the exhaust pipe.

These four strokes are the same in diesel-powered cars, which have "compression-ignition engines" that operate on a fuel-injected system. On the first or "intake" stroke only air enters the cylinder chamber. In stroke two, as with the gasoline engine, the piston moves up and compresses the air toward the top of the chamber. In stroke three, the "explosion" is not set off by a spark plug, but by the injection of fuel into the compressed hot air in the cylinder. Both the compression and injection actions create substantial heat, which sets off the explosion.

Some "high-performance" cars have turbochargers connected to their engines. Through the use of two fans, the turbocharger drives more air into the cylinders than the pistons would normally pull in themselves, allowing more fuel and air to burn and causing, in effect, a greater, more powerful explosion. Among the most controversial engine accessories, turbochargers can give big-car power to today's small engines, but add to the costliness of repairing the engine if it does fail. In addition, turbochargers themselves are very expensive to replace, $500 or more, and their pros and cons are worth thorough evaluation before you decide to buy a car that has one.

THE ELECTRICAL SYSTEM

The components of your electrical system give your engine the "spark" it needs to get going.

What happens when you turn your ignition key? Your *ignition switch* is connected to your *starter motor* by way of a *solenoid* (a wire-wrapped cylinder that conducts electricity). By turning the key you direct the solenoid to send electricity to the starter motor. The starter then turns a starter drive gear that spins the flywheel at the end of your engine, in turn causing your cylinders' pistons to move, and the four-stroke process to begin.

After the engine starts running on its own, engine power is transmitted to the *alternator* where it's turned into "electrical power." In turn, the alternator sends the electricity to your *battery* to keep it constantly charged, and to your lights, radio, and other electricity-dependent parts. The amount of electricity produced and distributed by the alternator is controlled by the *voltage regulator*.

When you turn your ignition key and send electricity to your starter, you simultaneously send electricity to your *distributor*, which rotates with the engine's crankshaft. The spinning

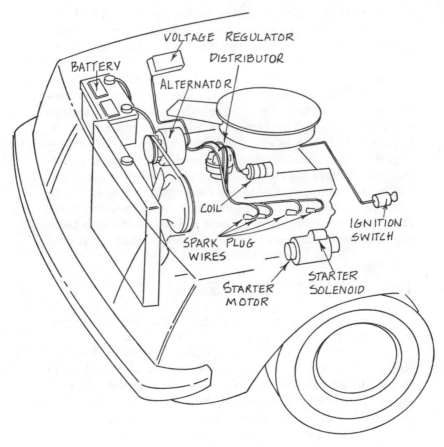

Electrical system

rotor inside the distributor sends the high voltage to each cylinder's *spark plug* in turn. The spark ignites the fuel/air mixture to cause the "power" stroke inside your engine cylinders.

For more information about the electrical system and some of the problems it may confront, see page 39 for how to check your battery; page 77 for what to do when your car won't start; and page 78 for how to jump-start a battery.

THE FUEL SYSTEM

The job of the components of your fuel system is to transfer the fuel from your *gas tank,* where gasoline is added when you "fill up" at a gas station, to the engine where it can be transformed into energy and the car can start.

The process begins with your *fuel pump,* usually located on the engine. The pump draws gasoline from your *gas tank,* usually located in the rear of your car, through the steel-tubed *fuel line* that runs the length of your car. When the gasoline arrives at the front of your car, it travels through a *fuel filter,* which removes sediment. From there, the gasoline travels up the fuel line toward the *carburetor* where it is mixed with air that's been cleaned, through the *air filter* seated on top of the carburetor, before it enters the carburetor. The *choke* restricts air flow into a cold engine. This restriction raises the percentage of fuel in the air/fuel mixture to ease starting and warm-up operation. (In diesel cars and other fuel-injected systems, fuel travels via the pressure of the fuel pump through a fuel filter and into a *fuel injector* that is attached to the engine.)

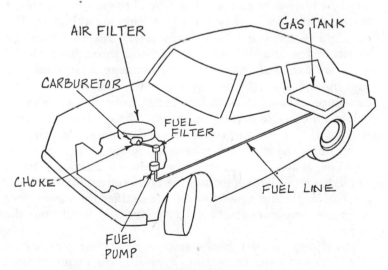

Fuel system

For more information on problems that can arise with your fuel system, see page 84 for the consequences of running on too-little gas; page 85 for what happens if you use the "wrong" octane fuel; and pages 86 and 88 for signs of leaks in your fuel system.

THE EXHAUST SYSTEM

Whenever something burns, two things happen: the burning creates some kind of energy, and when that energy is used up, the result is some sort of waste product. In your fireplace, the waste is ashes; in your car, the waste is exhaust gas, which begins in the exhaust stroke in your engine cylinders.

The exhaust stroke is the last stroke that occurs inside your engine; leftover gases are forced out of the cylinder chambers by pistons pushing upward. It is the job of the exhaust system to draw these gaseous waste products away from the engine, through a filtering system (the catalytic converter), and ultimately out of the car and into the air outside.

The process begins with your *exhaust manifold,* a device that is attached to your engine and has several openings that collect the exhaust gases as they leave your engine's cylinders. The manifold is connected to a sturdy *exhaust pipe* that runs the length of the underside of your car, and through which the gases are funneled. Along the exhaust pipe, the fumes first pass through a *catalytic converter*—standard equipment on most cars since 1975 when carmakers began using these devices to reduce undesirable exhaust emissions. The catalytic converter changes the carbon monoxide and hydrocarbons of your engine fumes into much less hazardous carbon dioxide and water. The fumes then reenter the exhaust pipe and travel through a *muffler,* which reduces the noise caused by the movement of exploding gases. Out of the muffler the fumes once again are sent through the exhaust pipe and finally out the *tailpipe.*

Sometimes exhaust fumes seep out of their combustion chambers and enter the engine, bypassing the manifold altogether. Over an extended period of time, this seepage could

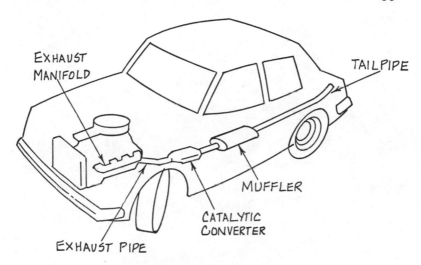

Exhaust system

cause rapid wear and ultimately engine failure. To avoid such problems, car manufacturers install *Positive Crankcase Ventilation (PCV)* systems in engines today. The system recycles the escaped gases and sends them back into the engine cylinder chambers to be reburned and redirected through the exhaust system. The *PCV valve* on the engine crankcase controls the amounts of escaped gases that are put back into the engine. This valve should be checked at every tune-up; a clogged PCV valve can lead to oil leaks into the engine or general build-up of sludge in the engine—both precedents of engine failure.

For more information on the exhaust system, see page 42 for how to check its components, and page 82 for problems with smoke from the car's tailpipe.

THE LUBRICATING SYSTEM

As you know, your oil is your car's most important lubricant and the main component of the lubricating system. It serves to

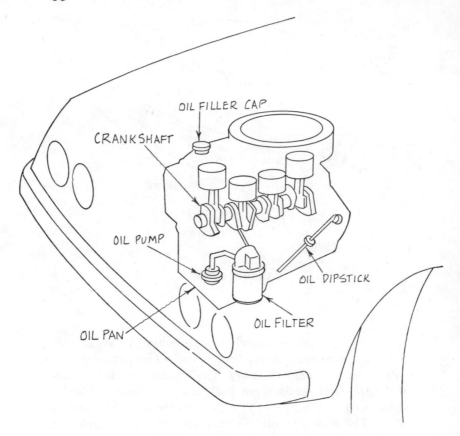

Lubrication system

cushion and cool automobile parts that otherwise would rub together and wear quickly.

Let's say that you've checked your oil level by looking at the oil *dipstick* and you've discovered you need to add a quart. When you pour oil in the oil-fill hole, it travels down into the *oil pan*. The oil is driven up to the moving engine parts by an *oil pump* that dips down into the oil pan. Before reaching the engine, oil passes through an *oil filter* that removes any sediment that could potentially wear against engine parts, then continues up into the engine where small passages send it circulating to all moving parts of your engine.

To learn how to check your oil, turn to page 21. For information on oil leaks and oil pressure problems, turn to pages 83, 86, 89.

THE COOLING SYSTEM

You've learned already how hot your engine can become under normal use—as hot as 5,000° F. To prevent your engine from burning up, this heat is cooled down, in a constant heat-removing cycle. Most cars' cooling systems consist of about ten components: thermostat, radiator, radiator cap, fan, fan clutch (or thermo switch), drive belts, hoses, coolant recovery system, water pump, and coolant.

While your engine is producing hot power inside its com-

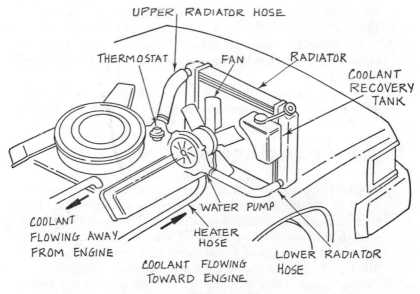

Cooling system

bustion chambers, the cooling system is sending coolant circulating around these chambers and valves to absorb the heat, and then sending it out through hoses to the radiator. The process starts from your *radiator.* Your radiator coolant is kept under pressure by the *radiator cap,* which seals off the radiator and raises the boiling point of the coolant, like a pressure cooker. Your *water pump* draws coolant from the radiator through the *lower radiator hose,* through which it travels to the engine. The coolant absorbs the engine heat and travels back toward the radiator through the *upper radiator hose.* Before it reaches the radiator, the coolant passes through a *thermostat,* a controller that keeps coolant temperature to no more than about 200° F. (safe operating temperature). The coolant is cooled in the radiator as the *fan* pulls cool outside air through the radiator, lowering the coolant temperature. The fan is driven by a *fan belt* or an electric motor; some fans also have a *fan clutch* that disconnects the fan when cooling is unnecessary to lessen the work for the engine.

Since coolant expands as it heats, a radiator that is full when cold will overflow when hot. To collect this "excess" coolant, most cars have a *coolant recovery tank* connected to the radiator. The coolant rests in this tank until it is sufficiently cool enough to be drawn back into the radiator through a vacuum action. (This recovery tank is the same place where you sometimes *add* coolant.)

For tips on what to do if your car overheats, and other problems with the cooling system, see pages 84, 87 and 119–21.

THE TRANSMISSION

When you *transmit* something, you send a message from one place to another. In the case of your automobile, the "message" that's being transmitted is power. The power that is created in the four-stroke process of your engine's cylinders requires the workings of the transmission system to spread to other parts of your car where it can be used.

Your transmission is connected on one side to the engine, and to the driveshaft on the other. Inside your transmission are a series of different-sized notched wheels known as *gears* (similar to the exterior setup of gears on a multispeed bicycle). When you shift gears in your car, you're moving from using one of these notched wheels to using another. Depending on where you're driving (uphill, downhill, level) and the speed at which you're driving, different gears will facilitate each motion.

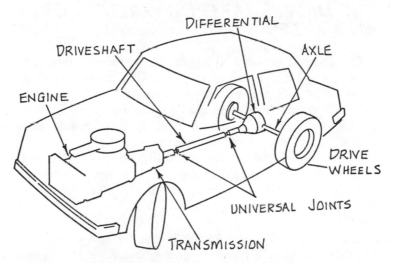

Transmission for rear-wheel drive

In automatic transmissions, your car "senses" its changing needs (e.g., more power and a lower gear if you're going uphill; less power and a higher gear if you're moving downhill) and changes gears automatically. Your automatic transmission fluid under pressure does the shifting while also lubricating and cooling the gears as they move.

In manual transmissions, the flywheel at the end of the transmission is attached to a clutch, which transfers the power coming from the engine, and which you control from a pedal beside your brake pedal. By pressing on the clutch pedal before changing gears, and holding it while you do, you're eliminating power being transmitted from the engine to the gears, and hence, preventing damage of gear parts (including actual break-off of gear teeth) as they are shifted into engagement by the driver moving the gearshift lever.

To learn how to check your transmission fluid, see page 31. For signs of—and possible solutions to—transmission problems, see pages 90–91 in the next chapter.

THE DRIVESHAFT, DIFFERENTIAL, AND AXLES

These three components are responsible for transferring the power created in your engine to your car's four wheels. In rear-wheel drive cars, the *driveshaft* is a rotating metal tube that transmits energy from the car's transmission to the *differential.* In turn, the differential is connected to the *rear axle,* which carries energy to the two rear wheels.

In front-wheel drive cars, the differential is incorporated into the *transmission* which is then called a *transaxle.* Power is carried from the transmission directly to the differential, which then splits the energy between the two front (or "driving") wheels.

The orientation of the engine in the car will often reflect whether you have a front- or rear-wheel drive car. In rear-wheel drive cars, the engine is set parallel to the driveshaft and perpendicular to the front of your car and the firewall. In front-wheel drive cars, the engine usually is in place "sideways"; that is, it is parallel to your front transaxle *and* parallel to the firewall and front of your car. In both cases, such placements allow the most direct transfer of power to the drive wheels.

For more information about possible problems with fluid leaks from this system, see the next chapter, page 88.

THE STEERING SYSTEM

All of the aforementioned systems help to give your car the energy it needs to get moving. But where you go depends on

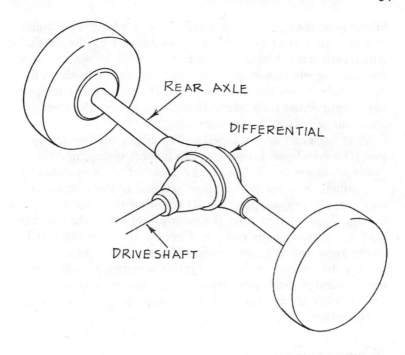

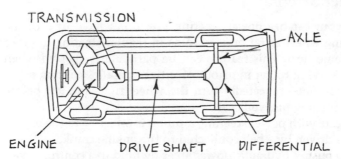

Driveshaft, differential, and axle for rear-wheel drive

how you steer. Your steering system is a set of mechanisms connecting your steering wheel to your tires.

Your *steering wheel* is attached to a *steering column*, which, in turn, is connected to a *steering gear*. If you drive one of the newer small cars, your car probably has *rack-and-pinion steering*.

In this case, the steering gear is called the "pinion." The pinion connects to a steel bar with notches known as the "rack," which connects the left and right front wheels. When you turn the steering wheel, you simultaneously cause the teeth on the pinion to turn on the teeth of the rack, causing the rack to move right or left (depending on the direction you're steering) and your wheels to do the same.

Most large cars are equipped with a *pitman arm* steering system. The *steering gear* is connected to a short metal link known as the *pitman arm* which, in turn, is connected to a perpendicular bar, called a *track rod.* A short link, parallel to the pitman arm, called an *idler arm,* supports the other end of the track rod. The turning signal is sent from the steering wheel to the steering gear, to the pitman arm and the idler arm, then simultaneously to the right and left front wheels. These "extra" linkages require extra room, which is why this steering system is not often found in small cars. This steering system acts to "cushion" vibrations from the road up through the steering column to the wheel.

Power Steering

If your car has power steering you don't have to turn the steering wheel as far or as hard as in regular steering to make the same turn. This feature can be particularly helpful when you're trying to get in or out of a tight parallel parking space and you must repeatedly turn the wheel right and left before straightening out your car.

In cars with power steering, a pump is attached to the engine and is driven by a belt connected to the engine crankshaft. The pump pushes hydraulic power steering fluid to a control device in the steering gear that determines how much fluid is needed to make a particular turn, then transfers that specific amount of pressurized fluid to help move the front wheels as the driver desires.

To learn more about possible problems and their solutions involving the steering system, turn to the next chapter, pages 89–90.

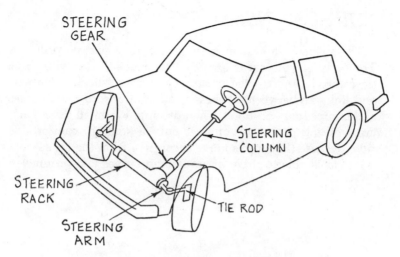

STEERING
GEAR

STEERING
COLUMN

STEERING
RACK

TIE ROD

STEERING
ARM

Rack-and-pinion steering

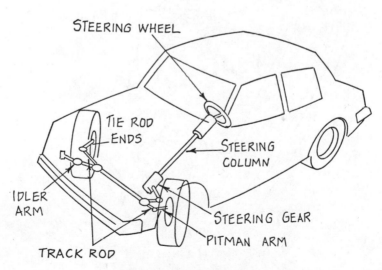

STEERING WHEEL

TIE ROD
ENDS

STEERING
COLUMN

IDLER
ARM

STEERING GEAR

PITMAN ARM

TRACK ROD

Pitman arm steering

THE SUSPENSION SYSTEM

The suspension system is the cushioning part of your car. The body of your car is literally "suspended" over your tires by carefully constructed groups of springs, shock absorbers, and linkages between all these parts that absorb the bounces and bumps you encounter when driving. When all these parts are working properly, you feel only a smooth, comfortable ride. Because the wheels move separately from the car's body, your car is able to drive around steep curves and on uneven

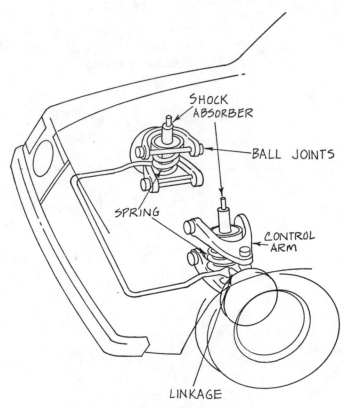

**Suspension system
(Front of car)**

land without toppling over. The suspension system adapts up to a point, so that one wheel can "grab" the lower ground while the other continues on the upper ground.

A typical suspension system includes *springs* (e.g., coil springs, leaf springs, or torsion bars), *shock absorbers, ball joints,* and *linkages.* The linkages keep the wheels in position as they move up and down over uneven road surfaces. The springs support the bulk of the weight of your automobile. Shock absorbers minimize the impact of road bumps on the springs. A relatively new mechanism on some cars called the "MacPherson Strut" combines the shock absorber and some of the locating linkages and corresponding ball joints into one part.

Each of these parts should be kept well lubricated with grease. (On some cars, these parts are permanently lubricated during manufacturing. Other cars need periodic regreasing, which is usually done during a "lube job" along with having the oil changed. See chapter one, page 24, for more details.) If some parts, such as pivots, are made of rubber, consult your owner's manual and confer with your mechanic about having these parts lubricated. Grease will cause the rubber to deteriorate. A silicone spray or special rubber lubricant might be needed instead.

To learn how to test your shock absorbers, turn to page 42. For further information about possible problems that can arise in the suspension system, see page 92.

TIRES

Besides providing the means by which a car can actually travel down the road, the tires and the wheels on which they're seated substantially affect the comfort you'll feel when sitting in a car, and its fuel efficiency. Unlike many other car parts, when it comes to *buying* tires, you have a great number of options. Different tire types offer different advantages and disadvantages. It's up to you to examine your own driving needs, and the requirements of your particular automobile, and decide which tire type is best for you. Since tires often last about 30,000 miles, there's a good chance that you'll have to replace your tires at least once during the life of your car. Knowing how tires are put together and being able to decode some of the mystifying symbols on a tire's sidewall will help you to make a wiser, more authoritative purchase.

Anatomy of a Tire

All tires consist of a rubber-covered strip of steel (the "bead") that forms an airtight seal around a metal wheel rim, and all tires have air valves, covered by removable caps, where you can check tire pressure and add or let out air as needed. From this point on, construction differs.

BIAS-PLY TIRES:

Bias-ply tires are generally the least expensive tires you can buy and have a lifespan of up to about 20,000 miles. These tires have two, four, or more layers (or "plies") of rubber-coated rayon, nylon, polyester, or other synthetic material that looks like a sturdy "canvas" material to the naked eye. The more plies that the tire has, the stronger it is. The plies are arranged on the tires in a kind of diagonal herringbone pattern, reaching from one edge of the bead to the other and set at about a forty-degree angle. These plies are then covered by rubber tire treads.

BELTED BIAS-PLY TIRES:

Belted bias-ply tires are slightly more expensive than simple bias-ply tires, but are expected to last 5,000 more miles, and may also pay off in added fuel efficiency. These tires are constructed the same as their bias-ply counterparts, but have an additional layer of material (belts) over the plies and under the treads. These belts improve the rolling resistance of tires, making them more fuel efficient, easier to handle through steering, and longer-lasting.

RADIAL TIRES:

Radial tires are fast becoming the most popular tire-replacement choice among car owners, and they are the predominant tires of choice by carmakers for their new products. Their con-

ANATOMY OF A TIRE

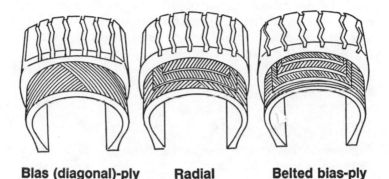

Bias (diagonal)-ply   **Radial**   **Belted bias-ply**

struction leads to a stiffer tread than bias tires, and hence results in longer tire life.

The plies in radial tires are made of a strong synthetic material, too, but they're laid out on the bead in a sort of monochromatic rainbow pattern, with each "ray" pointing toward the center of the bead as opposed to the angled bias pattern. The cords are then surrounded by a belt of woven fiberglass, or, in the stiffest case, woven steel.

Radial tires are generally best suited to "grip" the road, to provide good traction. This construction creates excellent all-around tires that will last some 40,000 miles and more. As could be expected, radial tires are generally the most expensive variety, but could pay off in better performance, fuel-efficiency, and longer tire life.

SNOW TIRES:

Snow tires are different from regular tires by reason of deeper tread depth with wider spaces between the blocks of tread rubber, which enables them to perform very well in mud and snow. However, they wear out faster and give poorer traction than regular tires on ordinary clear roads. For this reason, if you do use snow tires, you should never let them stay on your car past snow season. Like any replacement tire, snow tires should be the same type and size as your regular tires (i.e., if your regular tires are radials, your snow tires should be as well). While it is safe to use only two snow tires in areas of moderate snowfall (putting them on your driving wheels), four identical tires at any time offer best performance, especially on front-wheel drive cars.

See pages 124–25 for information about when to put snow tires on your car.

How to "Read" a Tire

Every car has certain specific requirements about the size and kind of tires that it can accommodate. Before you buy any replacement tires, you should examine the markings on the sidewalls of your current tires to find out the appropriate size and weight allowance. This information may also be available in your owner's manual or on the tire placard inside your doorjamb or glove compartment.

Starting with the outer perimeter of the tire, you'll find the manufacturer's name and the brand name of the tire.

Below the tire's name you'll see a letter and number configuration; a typical pattern might be: P 195/75R14. The "P" stands for "passenger," indicating that the tire is to be used on a standard passenger car, as opposed to a truck, bus, or other large vehicle. The next three numerals represent the width of the tire measured in millimeters (in this case the tire is 195 millimeters wide). The "75" is the ratio of the height of the tire to its width (in this case the tire's height is 75 percent of its width). The lower this number is, the wider and "squatter" the tire is; "60" is about the lowest number you'll commonly see in this spot. The "R" means this is a radial tire. You'd see a "B" in this spot if the tire was a belted bias-ply, or a "D" if the tire was a simple bias (diagonal)-ply.

In older tires, these figures are represented by alpha-numeric symbols *(see illus., p. 70)*. A typical marking might be: F 70 × 15. In this case, the "F" represents the amount of weight the tire can accommodate; the lower the letter of the alphabet (from F to A, for example), the smaller the size and load-carrying capability of the tire. The "70" represents the ratio of the

How to read a tire

tire height and width, and in this case means that the tire is 70 percent as high as it is wide. The second number indicates the diameter of the tire rim, in this case, fifteen inches.

The next row of information usually relates to the tire's construction—whether it's tubeless, the number of plies, and what their materials are (e.g., Tread 1 ply polyester + 2 plies fiberglass. Sidewall: 1 ply polyester). On this same line, you may also see the initials DOT, indicating that the tire meets the minimum safety standards, as set by the United States *D*epartment of *T*ransportation.

On the line closest to the center of the tire you may see numbers indicating the maximum weight allowance for this tire (e.g., Max Load 635 kg-1400 lbs) and the maximum inflation pressure.

**How to read a tire
(older numeric system)**

A Tire's Marks of Quality

On a tag or label attached to the tires in the shop and molded into the tire sidewall will be symbols rating the tire's tread-life, resistance to heat, and how well the tires maintain traction when braking on wet roads. This grading is done by the Uniform Tire Quality Grading System (UTQGS) using standards set by the federal government. For example, a really good tire might have a rating of 200 A/B. The "200" refers to the tire's tread life. Based on a standard road test course, the number represents an estimate of when the tires' treads will wear out on the test. Ten points is awarded for every 3,000 miles of predicted durability. A good tire will have a rating of at least "100" (indicating treads will last 30,000 test miles). In this example, "200" means that the treads would last about 60,000 test miles before wearing out. Your tires' tread life may differ depending on how and where you drive, and how well you maintain your car and your tires.

The first letter ("A" in this example) represents the tire's traction rating. All tires' tractions are rated A, B, or C—with "A" offering the best braking action on wet pavement, and "C" offering safe, acceptable traction, according to the Department of Transportation's standards for safety. Few tires are actually rated "C" for traction, so the choice, in fact, is between "A" as best and "B" as worst in the marketplace.

The second letter ("B" in this example) refers to the tires' resistance to heat that is created by the friction of the moving rubber on the pavement. Like the traction ratings, tires rated "A" are most heat-resistant, while those rated "C" meet minimum standards. These ratings are derived from a temperature-resistance test: in a simulated driving test, the tire is run for two hours at normal speeds, then run at a speed of at least 85 mph for thirty minutes (for a "C" rating) and up to 115 mph for thirty minutes (for an "A" rating). Since most drivers rarely attain these speeds, particularly for this amount of time, the heat-resistance rating is generally considered to be the least important of the three ratings. However, heat resistance also is a factor when driving a heavily loaded car or towing a trailer at highway speeds in hot weather.

To learn how to recognize the signs of tire problems—and their possible solutions—turn to page 92. For how to check tire pressure and how to add and let out air from your tires, see pages 10–12. Explanations of tire balancing and wheel alignment are provided on pages 15–18.

THE BRAKES

Each wheel has a brake behind it (which is why, in order to examine the brakes, your wheels have to be removed). Through the use of pressurized fluid, your brakes are responsible for stopping the motion of your wheels, hence stopping the overall motion of your car.

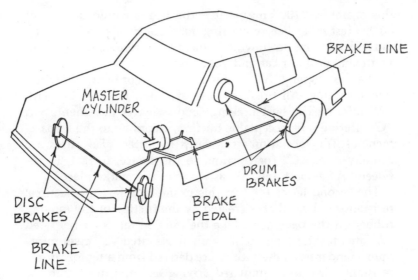

Brake system

Basically, there are two types of brakes: *drum brakes* and *disc brakes*. Most cars made today use both—disc brakes on the front wheels, and drum brakes on the back wheels—but there are exceptions. Some older cars have drum brakes on all four wheels, while some expensive cars have disc brakes on all four wheels.

All brake systems have the following components: brake pedal, master cylinder and brake fluid, brake lines, brake hoses, heat-resistant brake shoe linings (on drum brakes) or pads (on disc brakes), brake calipers (on disc brakes) or wheel cylinders (on drum brakes). Here's a concise explanation of how each of these parts work to make your car stop when you want it to.

When you want to stop your car, the pressure your foot exerts on the *brake pedal* causes the *master cylinder* (with a reservoir for brake fluid) to pressurize the *brake fluid* through the *brake lines* (steel tubing that runs from the master cylinder to all four wheels). The harder you press the brake pedal, the more fluid pressure and the faster you stop. The fluid then travels

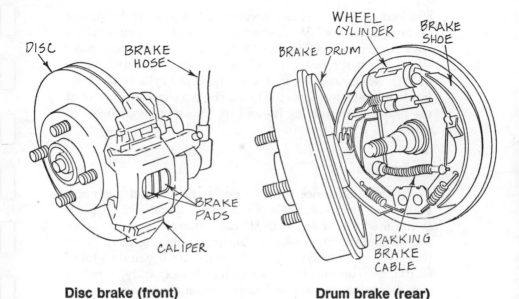

Disc brake (front)　　　　　　　**Drum brake (rear)**

through *brake hoses* that connect the brake lines to the brake *calipers* (on disc brakes) and *wheel cylinders* (on drum brakes). *Note:* Cars made today have dual-circuit master cylinders—really two separate systems in one assembly. One system usually services the rear brakes; the other, the front brakes. When you press the brake pedal, fluid is pressurized simultaneously to each set of brakes. However, if *one* of the systems has a leak, the other system should be unaffected so you should still have *some* braking power, though it will be weakened.

In disc brakes, the *calipers* look something like miniature fenders that arch over the top of the *disc* of the brake. Inside each caliper are two *brake pads,* one on either side of the disc. When you're driving, the disc rotates with your wheel. When you press the brake pedal, the hydraulic brake fluid travels through the system under pressure and forces pistons in the caliper to press the friction pads against the disc, causing the disc to stop moving, and hence, the wheels to stop moving as well.

In drum brakes, a hollow, shallow metal cup *(brake drum)* is attached to the wheel and revolves along with it. Inside the drum is a *wheel cylinder,* connected to two *brake shoes,* covered with friction material similar to that of the disc brake's pads. When the brake pedal is pushed and the pressurized brake fluid travels through the system to the wheel cylinders, pistons inside the cylinders force the brake shoes against the insides of the brake drum, causing it—and its corresponding wheel—to stop.

Power Brakes

The only difference between power brakes and nonpower brakes is a mechanism on the rod connecting the brake pedal to the master cylinder. This mechanism enables you to apply less pressure to the brake pedal, hence braking more easily (but *not* more quickly). It's a helpful feature if you do a lot of stop-and-go driving; your foot won't tire as quickly. Very few cars do not have power brakes as standard equipment now.

The Parking (or Emergency) Brake

The parking brake is a separate entity from the hydraulic braking system. Inside your car, it's either an extra pedal beside your regular brake pedal, or a lever between the front seats. If you've parked on a steep hill, you can either press this pedal all the way down, or pull the lever up to hold your car on the hill when you take your foot off the regular brake pedal. In so doing, you activate a system of cables and levers underneath your car that "lock" one pair of wheels in place (usually the rear wheels). This brake can also be a lifesaver in the rare event that you lose all power in your regular brakes during driving. As an emergency measure, you can pull up the lever or ease down the pedal to brake one set of wheels, bringing the car to a stop.

Antilock Brakes

In using the parking brake, you *want* to lock up your wheels, usually to prevent your car from rolling down a steep hill. But, there are times when you want to *prevent* your wheels from locking up, such as if you're in the middle of a skid on an icy surface.

Auto manufacturers are meeting this need with a feature called antilock brakes. In this system, when you press your brake pedal, a computer built into the brake system automatically senses the rotation of each wheel and automatically reduces the amount of pressure hitting the brake pads (and/or shoes) on any wheel that has locked and stopped turning. Antilock brakes are just beginning to become standard equipment on some luxury cars; but there's a good chance they'll become even more popular and common in the future.

For ways to recognize brake problems, and what to do about them, turn to the next chapter, page 91. For guidelines on how to check brake fluid, and how often to have brakes tested by a mechanic, see chapter one, page 40. For tips on the best ways to use your brakes in wet or snowy weather, see pages 118 and 126.

3
Trouble Signs and
What to Do About Them

By this point, you know how the systems of your car work and how to keep your car operating in peak performance through preventive maintenance. Yet, even the most pampered automobiles sometimes present problems. You can't be expected to be able to diagnose and fix your car's problems as if you'd gone through years of technical automobile training; but by knowing how your car runs, you should be able, at least, to narrow down the possible causes of trouble, and in some cases, you *will* be able to repair the problem yourself. While there's no way to outline all the possible problems that a car might have, here are some of the most common symptoms that car owners notice, and explanations of what some of their possible causes and solutions might be. The general categories that this chapter covers are:

GETTING STARTED

SITUATION: When you put your key in the ignition nothing happens; the key won't even turn.

POSSIBLE CAUSES/SOLUTIONS: If you can't at least *turn* the key in the ignition slot, your ignition lock or ignition antitheft device could be stuck. To release it, turn the steering wheel in the direction that the car's wheels are turned as hard as you can. (In these situations, the steering wheel can feel stiff and resistant to being turned.) With the steering wheel turned, try to turn your ignition key in the ignition switch. If it still won't turn, consult your owner's manual for ways to unlock the ignition.

SITUATION: The key turns in the ignition, but the engine doesn't turn over; all you hear is a deep murmur, followed by complete silence when you stop turning the key.

POSSIBLE CAUSES/SOLUTIONS: Your battery is probably dead. To find out for sure, turn on your headlights. If they look dim, or if they get dimmer when you use additional items like the horn, heater/defroster or radio—or if none of these additional items work properly—you probably have a dead battery.

Remember, a dead battery does not necessarily mean that the battery itself is faulty. The problem could be that your alternator isn't working properly and therefore not keeping the battery charged; or your voltage regulator may not be allowing enough electricity to be sent by the alternator to the battery. If your battery passes a "load" test (in which your mechanic notes whether the battery is taking a charge or not), the mechanic may want to examine the voltage regulator and alternator for problems, too.

Lift the hood of your car and examine the cables and clamps connected to your battery. Are the cable connections loose? Do the clamps look corroded? If so, they could be the cause of a dead battery.

To neutralize corrosion on battery clamps, use a small brush to apply a mixture of equal parts warm water and baking soda. Then, with gloves on your hands, try to jiggle the cables a few times to tighten the connections. After each time, step back from the car and have someone try to start the car again. (Note: Never have your hands on the cables while someone is trying to start the car; you could get an electrical shock.) Only try to start your car this way a couple of times; you could flood the engine (fill it with *too* much fuel) by doing it more. If the engine doesn't start when you've tried all the above methods, your car may need a jump start.

How to Jump-Start a Battery

Needing a "jump" to get a car started is particularly common on cold mornings. Batteries can supply less electrical power when the temperature gets low so that sometimes your battery needs some help from a second battery. Jump-starting your car provides that help. Electrical "jumper" or "booster" cables connect your battery to another car's stronger battery and the power runs from his to yours. *(See illus.,* pp. 80–81.)

BEFORE YOU USE JUMPER CABLES:
1) Make sure the battery is not frozen; if it is, don't attempt to jump-start it.
2) Have both cars within easy reach of each other, but not touching. You don't want to have to stretch the cables too far to attach them from one battery to another. Sometimes it's best to have the cars front end to front end; sometimes side by side works better.
3) Both batteries should be the same voltage—either six or twelve volts. Check both car owners' manuals to be sure.
4) Wear a pair of protective, flexible gloves, and, if possible, goggles over your eyes. Even "maintenance-free" batteries can give off explosive hydrogen gas, and in the rare case that there is an explosion, you want to be protected.
5) Make sure both cars are set in "Park" (or if one has a

manual transmission, in "Neutral") and that their parking brakes are set.

USING JUMPER CABLES:

1) When both cars are conveniently and safely parked, turn off the "good" car's engine and get your jumper cables ready to connect.

2) Look down on your battery for the positive (+) and negative (−) markings. These symbols or the letters "POS" and "NEG," like those on a flashlight battery, indicate that any battery needs two connections to make a complete electrical circuit. These symbols often correspond to the colors of the clamps at the ends of the jumper cables: red means positive, black means negative.

3) Take your red cable and attach it firmly onto the positive terminal of the dead battery. Next, attach the other end of the same red cable to the positive terminal on the good battery. Try to make sure that as much of the metal cable clamp as possible is in contact with the metal of the battery clamps to ensure electricity is conducted most efficiently. Next, attach one end of the black cable to the negative clamp of the good battery. *(See illustrations, pp. 80–81.)*

4) Now, here's the tricky part: attach the other end of the black jumper cable to a sturdy, nonmoving part of the engine of the car with the dead battery. Be sure that the cable is not lying across a part that moves when the engine runs. Don't be surprised when there is a small spark when you make this last connection.

5) Make sure that you do not mix up the cables, and wind up attaching the same cable to one negative and one positive terminal on the batteries. An explosion, an electrical shock to you, or damage to both batteries and the charging system of the car, could result. Never make both connections on one battery before moving to the other battery. It's too easy to get confused and make a dangerous mistake.

6) When all cables are securely fastened, walk over to the donor car and start it up, and let its engine run for ten minutes or so to charge up your dead battery.

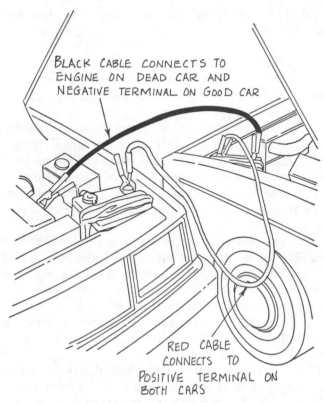

BLACK CABLE CONNECTS TO ENGINE ON DEAD CAR AND NEGATIVE TERMINAL ON GOOD CAR

RED CABLE CONNECTS TO POSITIVE TERMINAL ON BOTH CARS

Jump-starting a car

7) After allowing about five to ten minutes to elapse, try to start up your car, with jumper cables still attached. If it starts up, run the engine *lightly* at a normal fast idle speed to charge the battery even more. Let both cars run for another few minutes.

NOTE: If, after several minutes of charging the battery, your car still won't start—and you're sure the battery is dead—it's better to give up before you cause any damage to other parts of the car. It's possible that you could ruin the starter if you

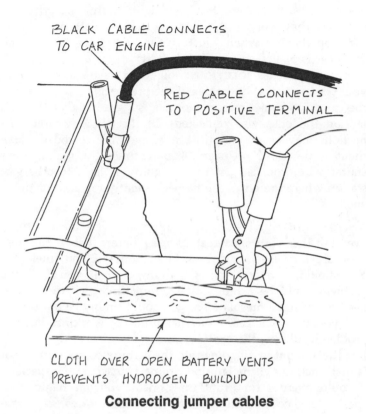

BLACK CABLE CONNECTS TO CAR ENGINE

RED CABLE CONNECTS TO POSITIVE TERMINAL

CLOTH OVER OPEN BATTERY VENTS PREVENTS HYDROGEN BUILDUP

Connecting jumper cables

continually try to start a car whose battery won't work.

8) Turn off the "good car." Carefully remove the negative cable from your car first, then from the donor's car. Then remove the positive cable from the donor car, then from your car.

9) If possible, try to get your car to a service station without driving too far on a jump-started battery. Have the station recharge your battery before your mechanic tests it to see if you need a new battery.

SITUATION: When you test your lights, horn, and other accessories, they work well, indicating that the battery is charging properly. But when you turn the key in the ignition, all you hear is a click; the car won't start.

POSSIBLE CAUSES/SOLUTIONS: You could have a loose wire in your starter (probably the case if the problem is intermittent—the car starts sometimes, not others, suggesting that through motion, the loose wire connected). Or, dirty battery cable connections may be the culprit, too. If they are corroded, clean them as described on page 78. Sometimes by jiggling your starter wire, you can get the car going at least to a service station where the wires can be permanently replaced or tightened.

SITUATION: You turn your ignition key and the car turns over, but then sputters and stops again before it stays running.

POSSIBLE CAUSES/SOLUTIONS: First, notice if you smell gas. You should, if everything is working well. If you *don't*, the problem could be a faulty fuel pump (in which case you'll need to consult a mechanic) or you could simply be out of gas.

If you do smell gas, your fuel pump is working, but the problem could be: the choke is sticking, not correctly controlling the amount of air going into the carburetor; the carburetor is malfunctioning; the ignition timing is inaccurate, especially if you're overdue for a tune-up. Consult your mechanic. Your spark plugs, coil, distributor cap, or ignition wires *(see illustration,* page 52) could be wet. If so, try to dry them with a towel.

SITUATION: The car backfires when you start it up.

POSSIBLE CAUSES/SOLUTIONS: If your car is equipped with an antibackfire valve, this mechanism could be at fault. If not, there's a malfunction somewhere in your emissions system, or distributor points could be worn out. Consult a mechanic.

SITUATION: Black smoke spews out of your car's tailpipe when you start up the ignition.

POSSIBLE CAUSES/SOLUTIONS: Your automatic choke or your carburetor could be malfunctioning, sending too little air or too much fuel to your engine (particularly likely if it's a cold morning). Consult your mechanic.

SITUATION: You're standing outside of your car and the hood

is up. Someone starts your car and you notice sparks flying around the engine.

POSSIBLE CAUSES/SOLUTIONS: Your spark plugs or ignition wires are worn. This could be due to long use, or it could signal a deeper problem. Sometimes worn spark plugs can indicate an internal oil problem, as oil will make spark plugs stop firing. After a mechanic removes the spark plugs, he will be better able to diagnose the cause.

SITUATION: On a nippy fall morning, you notice steam (not smoke) coming off your car's hood soon after you start driving; it stops after about five minutes of driving.

POSSIBLE CAUSES/SOLUTIONS: It's probably morning dew evaporating off the car's hood. Feel free to go on your way.

DASHBOARD WARNING LIGHTS

SITUATION: Your "Brake" light comes on as you're driving.

POSSIBLE CAUSES/SOLUTIONS: You're losing brake fluid or you already have lost part of your braking power. Pull into a service station as soon as possible to have brakes and fluid examined.

SITUATION: Your "Oil" light comes on when you're driving.

POSSIBLE CAUSES/SOLUTIONS: Your oil pressure is low, indicating oil is not reaching engine parts as it should and parts may be rubbing dry against each other. Low oil pressure could be caused by lack of oil, a clogged oil filter, or a failed oil pump. Whatever the reason, stop immediately. You may have already caused some damage to engine parts and if you continue to drive, you will quickly increase damage to parts that are costly to repair. Call for a tow truck to take you to a repair shop.

SITUATION: The "Battery" light goes on as you're driving.

POSSIBLE CAUSES/SOLUTIONS: Something is malfunctioning in your electrical system—probably your alternator, voltage regulator, or battery. Turn off all unnecessary equipment such as your heater/defroster; air conditioner; radio. Don't pull off the road unless you have to; once you turn off your engine, it may not start up again. Try to steer into the nearest service station for help.

SITUATION: Your "Coolant" light comes on when you're driving.

POSSIBLE CAUSES/SOLUTIONS: Your car may be on the verge of overheating. Pull over to the side of the road and try to find the cause of the problem: it could be a broken hose, a slipped fan belt, a defective radiator pressure cap—or lack of coolant. If low coolant is the problem, add some according to the directions on page 27. If the problem is a belt or hose or a defective radiator pressure cap, call for emergency road service. (See also page 119 for what to do if your car overheats.)

SITUATION: Your "Gas" light comes on when you're driving.

POSSIBLE CAUSES/SOLUTIONS: You're low on gas; although you could probably make it quite a few miles on what you have left, you'd be smart to fill up as soon as possible so that you're not running on the dirtier gas sucked up from the bottom of your gas tank.

NOISE WHILE DRIVING

SITUATION: You hear a rhythmic "thump" coming from one of your tires as you are driving.

POSSIBLE CAUSES/SOLUTIONS: You may have just run over a sharp object and your tire is losing air rapidly, turning "flat." Slow down and try to pull off the road to a safe, level spot. Follow the directions on pages 93–102 for how to handle a blowout or change a flat tire.

SITUATION: Your car starts well, but, in general runs poorly with hesitations, a lack of "pick-up," and noises.

POSSIBLE CAUSES/SOLUTIONS: Do you hear "pings" and "knocks" when you're driving? If so, think about the last time you filled up the gas tank. If you didn't buy high-octane gasoline, yet your car needs it, that could be your problem. Even if your owner's manual suggests that "regular" gasoline is good enough (and most new-car manuals do) as your car ages, its requirements can change. Switch to a higher-octane gasoline the next couple of times you fill up and see if the noises disappear. If they do, you've solved your problem.

If the noises don't disappear, consider whether you're driving with an unusually heavy load that could be putting stress on your engine. If your load is light, your problem could be somewhere else in the emissions system. Check your air filter to see if it's overfilled with dirt; if so, replace it. If it looks fine, have your mechanic check your carburetor and ignition to track down the problem.

SITUATION: As you're driving you hear a high-pitched squeal coming from under your hood; the more you accelerate, the louder the noise becomes.

POSSIBLE CAUSES/SOLUTIONS: You probably have a loose belt that could be driving your cooling fan, air conditioner, alternator, or power-steering mechanism. The longer you drive with this problem, the higher the risks that you'll wear out the belt completely or that you'll cause a more serious problem such as engine overheating (if it's the fan belt) or loss of battery charging and eventual loss of power (if it's the alternator belt).

Drive to a service station as soon as possible and have a mechanic change the loose belt. (If the car shows signs of overheating—see page 119—pull off the road, stop the car and wait for it to cool before trying to get to a service station.)

You can prevent this problem from occurring in the future by keeping steady tabs on the condition of all your engine belts. To learn how to do this, see page 36.

SITUATION: As you're driving you notice that the sounds from your exhaust pipe are getting louder and louder.

POSSIBLE CAUSES/SOLUTIONS: You may have a hole or other defect in your muffler or exhaust pipe, or these components may have become disconnected from each other. Have a mechanic certified in exhaust systems examine, and if necessary, replace these parts. In some cases, such problems may be simply more noisy than dangerous. But if the defect is in an area of the exhaust system that allows carbon monoxide to enter into the passenger section of the car, the consequences could be deadly; never let an exhaust system problem go unchecked.

SITUATION: Your tires squeal when you round curbs.

POSSIBLE CAUSES/SOLUTIONS: Your tires may be underinflated. Try not to drive too far before you park the car. Give the car at least an hour to cool down (longer depending on how far you've driven). Then check the tire pressure and add air if necessary (according to instructions on pages 10–12).

If the tire pressure is all right, consider whether you might have been driving faster than usual; driving around curves too quickly can cause tires to squeal. Tires may also squeal when you're driving over extremely smooth pavement; typically you might notice this sound in a parking garage, where the flooring is smooth, and the squeal can easily echo off of the ceiling and walls.

UNUSUAL ODORS

SITUATION: You smell "something burning" coming from under your hood while you're driving.

POSSIBLE CAUSES/SOLUTIONS: Look for any signs of smoke coming from under your hood and pull off the road if you notice smoke, or if the smell persists or grows stronger. A fire can be set off by any number of problems, but a fuel leak is the most common. Once you have pulled off the road, feel the hood before opening it. If the hood is extremely hot, be very careful that flames do not flare up as the hood is raised.

If there is a fire, don't use water to put it out; the fire could be caused by an oil leak and water would only spread the oil and consequently the fire. Use a fire extinguisher, dirt, or sand to put out the fire, or smother it with a fire-resistant blanket. Sometimes the exhaust fumes of other cars can take on a burning odor when you're behind them; so smelling "something burning" is not always a cause for concern.

SITUATION: You smell a hot, "chemical" burning smell from under your hood.

POSSIBLE CAUSES/SOLUTIONS: In rare cases, if you have a radiator leak, and antifreeze drips out onto hot parts of the engine (such as parts of the exhaust system), the quick evaporation of the antifreeze can cause this kind of burning smell. If you suspect this might be the case, monitor your radiator fluid level carefully, and if you seem to be losing an unusual amount of fluid, have the cooling system checked by a specialist.

SITUATION: You smell "something burning" from the direction of your back or front wheels.

POSSIBLE CAUSES/SOLUTIONS: Check to see if you might have left your emergency brake on. Sometimes, if it's on just a little bit, and you drive even a short way, the friction of the emergency brake and the wheels (usually your rear wheels) can cause excessive heat and create a burning smell. Stop the car and turn the emergency brake all the way off.

If the cause isn't your emergency brake, consider whether you're driving in mountainous territory, or whether you're towing an unusually heavy load, or whether you've been putting unnecessary stress on your brakes by stopping and going in spurts. All of these factors can cause a situation known as "brake fade," the overheating of brakes due to overuse; the smell will be accompanied by weakening brake power, causing you to have to press harder on the pedal in order to stop the car.

If possible, get on level ground, out of traffic's way, stop the car, and get out and carefully put your hand on the hubcap of the wheel from which the burning smell is coming. If the hubcap feels hot, you've been overusing your brakes and they've overheated. Simply pull over to the side of the road and let them cool down (to the point where the hubcap feels cool). This should solve the problem, but to be on the safe side, test the brakes out while you're still on a quiet, level street, while driving slowly. If you still have little brake power, have them checked by a brake specialist.

SITUATION: You smell gas as you're driving.

POSSIBLE CAUSES/SOLUTIONS: You probably have a leak somewhere in your fuel system—especially if you've had to fill up the gas tank more frequently than usual. Have your fuel system checked by your mechanic.

SITUATION: You notice a "rotten egg" smell inside your car.

POSSIBLE CAUSES/SOLUTIONS: It is likely that you have a car with a catalytic converter, and the fuel system is sending an incorrect mixture of air and fuel to the engine. Your gas mileage may be lower than usual, too. Have a mechanic find the cause—possibly the carburetor needs adjusting—and the smell will be gone.

FLUID LEAKS

SITUATION: You notice a small puddle of yellow-greenish fluid in the driveway below where you parked your car last night.

POSSIBLE CAUSES/SOLUTIONS: Your coolant is leaking. Look to see if the radiator hoses have burst, or if a clamp that holds the hose in place has loosened. If so, you could try to fix the hose temporarily, using a new clamp (which you should keep in your trunk) to secure the hose to its connection until you can drive to a nearby service station to have it replaced permanently. If the hoses look all right, your radiator could be cracked, or its petcock could be dripping. If the petcock is okay, fill the radiator with more coolant (you should keep some in your trunk) and drive as soon as possible to a service station to have the problem checked out professionally.

SITUATION: You notice brownish-black liquid on the parking spot you're pulling out of.

POSSIBLE CAUSES/SOLUTIONS: Is it between your car's rear wheels? If so, your car could be leaking rear-axle/differential fluid. If not, it's probably an oil leak. In either case, drive your car immediately to the closest mechanic.

SITUATION: You notice a puddle of reddish fluid under your parked car.

POSSIBLE CAUSES/SOLUTIONS: Your automatic transmission fluid or your power steering fluid is leaking. Check the levels of both *(see illustration,* p. 31) and get the car to a service station as soon as possible.

SITUATION: While bending to look under your car, you notice drops of clear liquid in your driveway.

POSSIBLE CAUSES/SOLUTIONS: Before going near the liquid, look at your car's battery. If you see cracks in the battery or if the battery caps have popped off, and the clear liquid puddle appears on the ground below the battery, assume the liquid is leaked battery acid. *Don't go near it.* Consult your mechanic; you'll probably need a new battery.

If the battery looks normal and the puddle is nowhere near the battery, the clear liquid is either condensation from your air conditioner or the morning dew. You can drive off safely.

STEERING PROBLEMS

SITUATION: As you're driving, the steering wheel gradually gets "stiff" in your hands and won't turn easily.

POSSIBLE CAUSES/SOLUTIONS: First, look for any warning lights on your dashboard. Sometimes, stiff steering can be a sign that your car has stalled, in which case you should put the car in "neutral" or "park" and try to start it again.

If your car has definitely not stalled, you might have a power steering fluid leak, or the belt driving the power steering pump might have broken. If the steering is almost impossible to control, switch on your "hazard" lights, slow down, and try to make your way to the nearest service station. The mechanic will most likely find the source of the leak or the broken belt.

SITUATION: The car pulls to the right or left as you're driving.

POSSIBLE CAUSES/SOLUTIONS: If it happens when you momentarily let go of the steering wheel as you're driving, the problem is most likely that your front wheels are out of alignment. Have your mechanic test the alignment.

SITUATION: The steering wheel "shimmies" back and forth as you drive.

POSSIBLE CAUSES/SOLUTIONS: Your front wheels are probably out of balance or your shock absorbers may be worn out. (If your front seat is vibrating, your back wheels are out of balance.) In either case, have your mechanic check, and if necessary, balance your tires, or replace your shock absorbers.

SWITCHING GEARS

SITUATION: You have an automatic transmission and the car doesn't move when you switch into "Drive."

POSSIBLE CAUSES/SOLUTIONS: First, make sure you've put the selector lever squarely into "Drive," and not between positions, which could cause the engine to race. Next, make sure your parking brake is not on. Once both these causes are eliminated, the problem could be too little transmission fluid; check it according to the directions on page 31. If the transmission fluid level is all right, the problem could be that the transmission needs adjusting. Check with a transmission specialist.

SITUATION: In your automatic transmission, the gears shift roughly and jerkily.

POSSIBLE CAUSES/SOLUTIONS: Most likely, your transmission fluid is low; check it. If that's not the problem, parts that control shifting within the transmission need adjusting or replacement.

SITUATION: Your clutch sticks; it's difficult to change gears and the clutch "rattles" when in gear.

POSSIBLE CAUSES/SOLUTIONS: Parts within the transmission could be worn. Another possibility is wear in the clutch operating mechanism. Have this problem checked out by a technician certified to work on transmissions.

BRAKE PROBLEMS

SITUATION: You hear a loud "grinding" sound when you apply your brakes.

POSSIBLE CAUSES/SOLUTIONS: Your brake pads (in disc brakes) and/or shoes (in drum brakes) are worn to a point where their metal base is scraping against the metal of the brake disc and/or drum. Have your brake pads checked and replaced *immediately.*

SITUATION: You hear "squeaks" when you apply the brakes.

POSSIBLE CAUSES/SOLUTIONS: A brake pad may be loose or rusty, causing it to vibrate and squeak when the brakes are applied. Have your car's brakes professionally examined.

SITUATION: You have to press your brake pedal all the way down to get any brake response; and the car takes a long time to stop.

POSSIBLE CAUSES/SOLUTIONS: Your brake fluid is leaking, so there's not enough hydraulic pressure on the pads and/or shoes to enable them to make the wheels stop. This often is accompanied by a warning light shining on the dashboard. Don't drive for long in this situation; get the car to a service station where a professional can find and fix the leak.

SITUATION: You have to "pump" the brake pedal to get the car to stop.

POSSIBLE CAUSES/SOLUTIONS: Either there's air in the brake lines; you're low on brake fluid; or one side of your dual master cylinder is leaking. Check the fluid level yourself. (See page 30 for instructions.) If the brake fluid reservoir is at a low level, add fluid. See a mechanic who can examine the car thoroughly for leaks, whenever this or any brake problem arises.

SITUATION: The car pulls to the right or left side as you're braking.

POSSIBLE CAUSES/SOLUTIONS: If this happens when you're braking, your brakes could be stopping the wheels unevenly. Have your mechanic examine the problem. If your car pulls sideways and you've recently driven over a sharp object, pull off the road slowly and check your tires to make sure they're not losing air.

SITUATION: Your car has disc brakes; when you apply the brake pedal, it vibrates up and down.

POSSIBLE CAUSES/SOLUTIONS: The "disc" part of your brake is warped so the brake pads can't close completely. Have your mechanic inspect the discs. Sometimes, they can be refinished to a flat surface again. When badly damaged, your brakes should definitely be replaced.

TIRE AND SUSPENSION PROBLEMS

SITUATION: When you're driving, the ride seems unusually bouncy, and you continue to feel the effects of each bump long after it is left behind.

POSSIBLE CAUSES/SOLUTIONS: Your shock absorbers are most likely worn out. To test them, stand outside your car and press down on the hood first, then on the trunk. If the car bounces more than once either time, your shocks probably need· replacement. Have them checked by a professional.

SITUATION: You hear a "clicking" sound coming from one tire as you're driving.

POSSIBLE CAUSES/SOLUTIONS: Probably a pebble or other small object is caught in the tread. Check to make sure. A rhythmic "thump" sound coming from your tire may mean your tire is rapidly losing air. If so, pull off the road and follow the instructions on pages 93–102 regarding tire blowouts and how to change a tire.

SITUATION: While examining your tires, you notice a bulge or lump in one of them.

POSSIBLE CAUSES/SOLUTIONS: Your tire's plies might be separating. Have a tire specialist look your tire over and if necessary, replace it before it causes a blowout.

SITUATION: Your tires seem to be wearing out more quickly in the middle than on the sides.

POSSIBLE CAUSES/SOLUTIONS: They're overinflated. Check the air pressure and let some air out, if necessary. (See directions on page 10.)

SITUATION: Your tires are wearing out more quickly on the edges than in the center.

POSSIBLE CAUSES/SOLUTIONS: They're underinflated. Check the air pressure and add air, if necessary. Tire blowouts are more likely to occur if tires are underinflated, so check their inflation periodically.

SITUATION: Only one side of your tires appears worn.

POSSIBLE CAUSES/SOLUTIONS: Your tires are out of alignment, or something is amiss in your suspension system. Have them examined by a professional.

SITUATION: Every time you check tire inflation, one tire always needs more air.

POSSIBLE CAUSES/SOLUTIONS: There's a slow leak either in the tire itself or in its air valve. Examine the tire for embedded objects, and put your ear by the air valve to note if you can hear air escaping. If you can't find the problem, have your tire expert remove the tire and examine it. Have it repaired if possible; replace it if it's beyond repair.

Tire Blowouts

Tire blowouts, like an overheating engine, can occur in any type of weather; but they're most likely to happen when you're driving a long distance at high speeds, and especially, if your tires are *under*inflated. Being underinflated causes a tire to become "flabby" and the rubber to flex excessively as you drive, causing the air inside the tire to heat and expand rapidly. If you are towing a heavy load, remember to inflate your tires to the maximum pressure on your inflation label (see page 69). A blowout can also result from a puncture to the tire and the loss of air as you drive. (Both are good reasons to check your tire treads *and* inflation every morning before heading out on a trip.)

WARNING SIGNS AND HOW TO RESPOND

☐ Your tires will usually warn you of an impending blowout in one of two ways: 1) You may hear a rhythmic "thump" as you drive, caused by a bulge in the tire; or 2) Your car will pull sideways if you've recently run over a sharp object and your tire is losing air rapidly. In either case, try to pull off the road slowly to a safe spot to change the damaged tire *before* it collapses completely. (See below for how to change a tire.)

☐ If your tire unexpectedly blows out, throwing the car out of control, resist the urge to slam on your brake pedal. Instead, calmly hold tight to your steering wheel and gently ease up on your accelerator. Then *slowly* apply the brake pedal and try to turn the car off the road onto the highway breakdown lane. Turn on your "Hazard" flashers as soon as you feel in complete control of the car again.

How to Change A Flat Tire

Once you're on the side of the road, out of the way of on-coming traffic, park your car and put on the parking brake. Make sure everyone is out of the car and that your car is parked on hard, level ground. If it is *not*, don't attempt to change the flat; the jack could easily sink into the soft earth, or the car, on slanted ground, could topple off the jack, presenting serious danger to you, passengers, and the car itself.

If you are parked on a safe, level surface, you should be able to change the tire yourself. Here are step-by-step instructions:

BEFORE YOU USE THE JACK (pp. 95–97):

1) Be sure that the parking brake is on, and the transmission is in "park" (automatic) or first gear (manual).

2) For added protection, place rocks, bricks, or heavy planks of wood in front of the two front tires and the nonflat rear tire (if you're changing a flat rear tire), or behind the two back tires and nonflat front tire (if you're changing a front flat). These extra "anchors" will help to prevent the car from rolling off the jack. *(See illustration below.)*

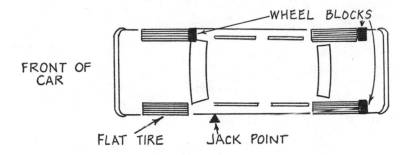

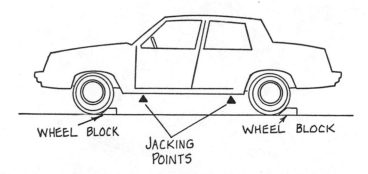

3) Remove all the equipment you will need from the trunk—including spare tire, jack, and toolbox (or at least a cross-type lug wrench and screwdriver). You should not plan to go into your trunk once the car is up on the jack; doing so could shake the car, causing it to drop off the jack.

4)   Use a screwdriver or other tool recommended in the own-er's manual to remove the hubcap off the flat tire. *(See illustration below.)*

5)   Using a wrench (preferably a cross-type lug wrench that gives extra turning power), loosen the lug nuts on the tire by turning them counterclockwise, until they require little effort to remove—but don't remove them completely. If you wait until the car is jacked up to do this, a hard jerking motion on the wrench could cause the car to drop off the jack. *(See illustration at right.)*

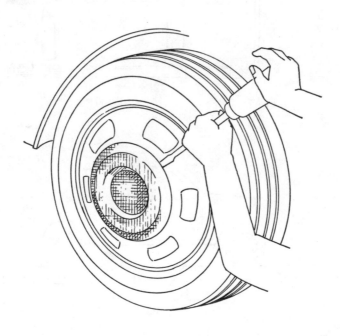

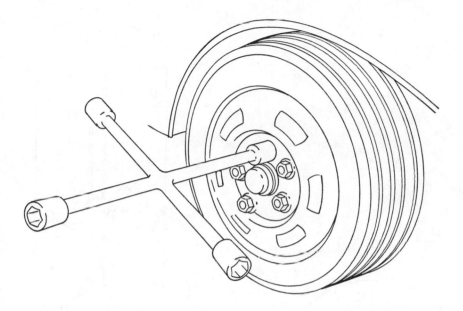

USING THE JACK (pp. 97–102)**:**

1) Most large cars come equipped with a "bumper" jack, which is generally thought to be easier to use than the scissors jack that comes with most small cars today. In either case, carefully follow the instructions for assembly and use, located either in your car owner's manual or on the jack container itself.

2) Once the jack is securely in position, jack the car up so the tire is about three inches off the ground. *(See illus.,* p. 98.)

WARNING: Never get under the car once it's on the jack since the car could slip off and injure you.

3) Remove the tire's lug nuts with your fingers (as shown on p. 100) and put them in your pocket so you won't lose them.

4) Get a solid grip on the flat tire and pull it straight off the threaded studs in a strong, direct motion. *(See illus.,* p. 99.)

5) Lay the flat tire under the side body of your car. This way, if the car does drop off the jack, landing on the tire will prevent the car from falling completely and injuring you or making it impossible to jack up again. *(See illus.,* p. 99.)

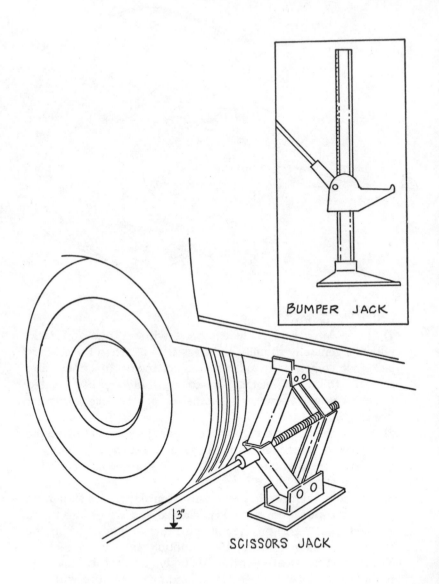

BUMPER JACK

3"

SCISSORS JACK

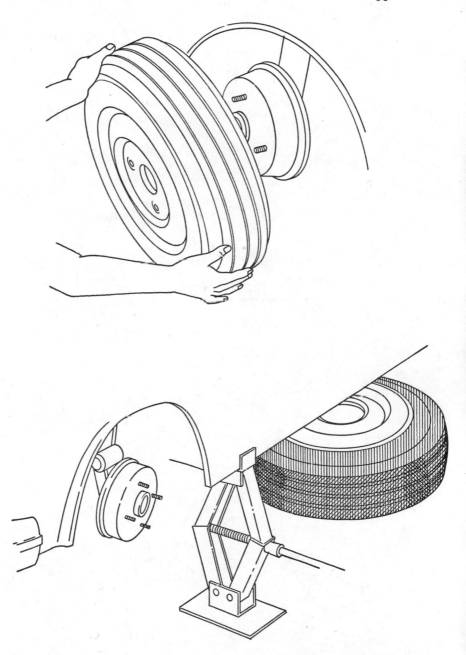

PLACE
BEVELED SIDE
OF NUTS
TOWARD THE
WHEEL

1-2"

6)   Gently put the spare tire on the axle, trying not to disturb the precarious position of the car on the jack.

7)   Twist the lug nuts in place with your fingers. Wait until the car is lowered to the ground before tightening them completely. *(See illustration on facing page.)*

8)   Remove the flat tire from under the car.

9)   Gently use the jack to lower the car until your tire is barely touching the ground. *(See illustration on facing page.)*

10)   Using your wrench, turn each lug nut clockwise until it is secure. Tighten lug nuts in the order shown. *(See illustrations below and on next page.)*

11)   Lower the car to the ground, remove the jack, and mustering as much strength as possible, give the lug nuts a final

Sequence to ensure even bolt tension

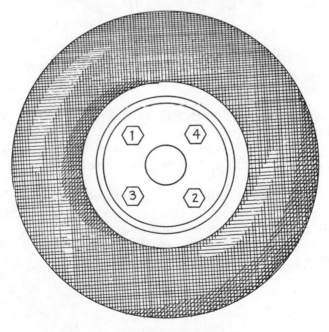

4-lug wheel

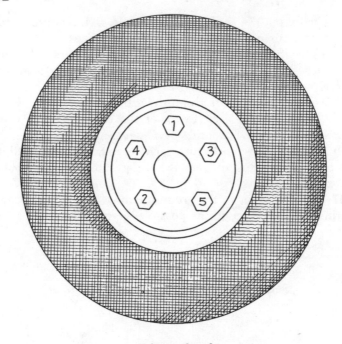

5-lug wheel

turn with the wrench to make sure they won't loosen as you're driving.

12)   Replace the hubcap and put all your equipment back into your trunk including, of course, the flat tire.

Today, many spare tires (especially those that don't look the same as the other four tires on your car) are meant to be used only for a short time. As soon as possible, get to a service center and either have your regular tire repaired or, if it's severely damaged, replaced.

4
Finding a Mechanic You Can Trust

In addition to the special care and preventive maintenance you give your car, your car's best friend is a reliable, competent mechanic. Few situations are as disheartening as discovering that a repair for which you paid a lot of money does not really fix your car.

Sometimes such a mishap can't be avoided; a real solution can only be found through trial-and-error of other possible solutions. But often a more skilled mechanic with up-to-date tools might have been able to diagnose and solve your car's problem the first time around, preventing extra costs and stress for you.

With cars becoming more sophisticated, and the cost of labor rising ever-higher (the price depending on where you live, the type of shop you go to, and the experience of the mechanic), finding a trustworthy mechanic and shop can be a more challenging—yet ultimately worthwhile—task than ever before.

WHAT ARE YOUR CHOICES?

In the old days of small towns and general stores it was easy to know where to bring your car when it needed fixing; you went to the local auto repair shop down the street. As long as the job wasn't too complicated, you could bet that the hometown mechanic would do good work at a fair price; after all, his local reputation was at stake and he wanted you, and other townspeople, to come back again.

Today you have many more choices of types of auto repair shops and consequently, more opportunity to find a mechanic with more expertise; or, on the other hand, someone who's not quite as reputable as he should be.

Some factors that can affect where you take your car for service and repairs include: what you're willing to pay, what repair is necessary, the recommendations of friends, and your own instincts. Here's a rundown of some options that are available and the advantages and disadvantages of each.

DEALERS:

The service, parts, and repair departments of the dealerships where you bought your car.

POSSIBLE ADVANTAGES:

□ If your car is under warranty with this dealer, most repairs will be made free of charge.

□ If your car is a new model, the dealer is more likely to have specific new parts and be aware of specific problems common in your make of car.

□ A business relationship already exists between you and the dealership; if they want you to buy cars from them in the future, they might be more likely to do a good job today.

□ Patronizing the same dealer for many years means they might give you a better trade-in value when it comes to buying a new car.

POSSIBLE DISADVANTAGES:

□ Once your warranty expires, repairs at a dealer can be more costly than at other shops. Their overhead cost is higher than smaller shops so you may be paying not only for your repair, but a fraction of your bill may go to paying the dealer's advertising costs, public relations bills, etc.

☐ In most dealerships you rarely get to meet the actual mechanic who works on your car. Transactions are performed through a service advisor who acts as a mediator between you and the mechanic and draws up a "repair order" (RO).

☐ In some places, insurance laws or company rules don't permit you to see the garage in which your car is being serviced.

DEPARTMENT STORES' AUTO REPAIR SHOPS:

Sears, Montgomery Ward, K-Mart, and other department or chain stores offer automotive services.

POSSIBLE ADVANTAGES:

☐ These shops usually offer services less expensively than dealerships.

☐ They are generally open longer hours, often including weekends.

☐ Such shops are conveniently located, often in shopping malls, so you can take care of other errands on foot while your car is being repaired.

☐ They often offer "specials" on certain services, such as tune-ups, brake jobs, oil changes, and muffler replacements.

POSSIBLE DISADVANTAGES:

☐ Sometimes those "specials" they advertise can be lures; once you get into the shop, you discover that the special-priced muffler replacement doesn't fit your particular make of car—and the one that does is four times the price. But since you're there anyway, you might decide to leave your car in the shop to save more inconvenience.

☐ As in dealerships, often you don't get to meet and evaluate the mechanic who actually works on your car.

SPECIALTY SHOPS:

Some places specialize in one or two areas of auto repair—

commonly, brakes, oil changes, muffler, transmission, or tires.

POSSIBLE ADVANTAGES:
☐ Like the chain stores, specialty stores sometimes offer periodic "deals" and lower prices on specific repairs.

☐ They often have at least one mechanic on staff certified in the particular area of specialty.

☐ Their hours and locations are generally convenient.

POSSIBLE DISADVANTAGES:
☐ Since you often don't get to meet the mechanic who'll be working on your car, you won't know for sure if that person is certified in the area of repair that your car needs.

☐ Some specialty shops have a reputation for getting you to buy more than you need. They may lure you with a "loss leader item," such as a $12.95 muffler; and after your car is up on the lift, they might say something like "After checking your car over and discovering that your car has a dented catalytic converter and a corroded tailpipe, we recommend installing an entire new exhaust system." So, a $12.95 muffler may turn into a $200 repair. (A precaution you can take is to examine your car before you bring it into the shop, so, for example, you have an idea just how corroded your tailpipe really is. Once in the shop, be firm in your instructions that *no* additional work should be done on your car without your permission.)

SERVICE STATIONS:
Many gasoline stations also offer on-location repairs by a full-time staff mechanic.

POSSIBLE ADVANTAGES:
☐ Such service stations usually offer lower-priced repairs.

☐ They're conveniently located, and offer an easy "neighborhood" atmosphere in which to develop a working relationship.

□ You can get to know the station owner, mechanic, and/or service help not only by going there for repairs, but by filling up at the gas pump. Usually you can get a good idea of how organized and dedicated the workers are by looking in the garage.

POSSIBLE DISADVANTAGES:
□ While individual repairs may cost less, a small station may be less likely to have the most current diagnostic equipment, so a problem might take longer to be recognized and repaired.

□ In a small service station, sometimes with a one-man staff, you're relying on a certain mechanic's expertise, unlike larger shops where a mechanic can confer with other more skilled colleagues to find and repair a problem.

PRIVATE AUTO-REPAIR GARAGES:
These shops are privately owned (frequently by an on-staff mechanic) and often specialize in one type of car make.

POSSIBLE ADVANTAGES:
□ There's usually a great chance for direct contact with the mechanic who'll be working on your car, and opportunities to check out the condition of the garage.

□ Often, you can find a shop that specializes in your model car, is familiar with associated common problems, and is well stocked with usual car parts.

□ You may get all the above benefits at a cost that is lower than that of a dealership (once your warranty runs out).

□ The owner of such a shop is often more concerned about his reputation in the community than larger shops might be, so he may be more likely to do finer-quality work.

POSSIBLE DISADVANTAGE:
□ High-quality private repair garages are rare, and hard to

find; personal recommendations and general community reputations are good clues to finding a good auto-repair shop. Generally, if you live in a small community, and the shop's been in business successfully for many years, there's a good chance it's an honest quality place; tight-knit communities don't tolerate highway robbers for very long.

SUGGESTIONS FOR FINDING A RELIABLE REPAIR SHOP

The previous guidelines can give you a good general idea of the differences in service that exist among various kinds of auto-repair shops. But obviously, they can't tell you if a shop is going to be fair, honest, and reliable. You must find that out for yourself.

☐ *Don't* wait until you need a repair to go looking for a shop. You're likely to be anxious and worried about the safety of driving your car, and the costs of repairing it, and you're more likely to trust the first person you go to, rather than doing some smart comparison shopping.

☐ Seek out a repair shop shortly after you buy a car, or at least after the warranty runs out, if you no longer plan to go to your dealer for service. You can "test out" a repair shop on small jobs first, such as replacing a fuse or spark plug; if the small jobs go off without a hitch, you can have *some* assurance that the large, expensive jobs will, too.

☐ Find out the reputation of the shop from friends and neighbors.

☐ Call your local Better Business Bureau, and ask if any complaints have been filed against the shop in question. The Better Business Bureau won't pass judgment on the shop *per se,* but will let you know about the shop's track record.

☐ Check out the shop's setup. A garage should be organized

and systematic in appearance, and the mechanics should at least *look* busy. (You don't want to pay someone on a per-hour basis if he's going to stand around idly.)

☐ Compare the equipment each shop you're considering uses. You can't be expected to know and recognize the latest diagnostic equipment, but you should ask each shop owner what equipment he has available and how it helps in diagnosis and time-saving. As a rule, shops should have at least two lifts and the mechanics should be working with the most up-to-date repair manuals available.

TWO GOOD SIGNS TO LOOK FOR:

1) *"We employ technicians certified by the National Institute for AUTO-MOTIVE SERVICE EXCELLENCE. Let us show you their credentials."* The National Institute of Automotive Service Excellence (ASE) certifies auto technicians (or mechanics) in one—or all—of eight different areas: engine repair, automatic transmission/transaxle, manual drive train and axles, suspension and steering, brakes, electrical systems, heating and air conditioning, engine performance. Body repair and painting/refinishing certifications are also offered.

To be eligible for certification, a technician must first have two years of practical experience (or one year's experience plus completion of courses in accredited trade and vocational schools) *and* must pass an extensive written exam in each automotive category. Once certified in one to seven specialties, the technician receives a silver patch (to be worn on his uniform) that states that he is ASE-certified. Technicians who are certified in all eight areas are recognized as "master automobile technicians" and receive a gold patch instead of the silver one. In addition, to maintain their certificate, technicians must be retested every five years to ensure they're keeping up with technological changes in their particular specialty.

Shops with ASE-certified employees usually hang their certificates in the shop's waiting room, and hang a blue-and-white sign outside their shop that says they employ ASE-certified technicians.

A few words of caution: if a shop displays the ASE sign, it does not mean that all its employees are ASE-certified; only one has to be in order for them to hang the sign. It's up to you to request that your car be worked on by a certified technician. It's also up to you to double-check that the mechanic working on your car is certified in the area on which he's working. (ASE does not guarantee, for example, that a technician certified in brakes, steering, and electrical systems is going to do a good transmission overhaul on your car.)

2) *"AAA Approved Auto Repair":* The American Automobile Association (AAA) approves the shop in which NIASE automotive technicians work. Since 1975, AAA has established a set of standards that repair shops must meet in order to receive the AAA sign of approval. AAA-approved repair shops must offer a minimum of services including: engine tune-up, minor engine repair, brake and electrical services, and either suspension and steering, or heating and air-conditioning services.

In addition, AAA personnel inspect each prospective shop to ensure the following:

—that the staff wears proper identification, is courteous, qualified, and efficient, and that customer facilities are clean, safe, and comfortable.

—that the garage itself is clean, uncluttered, and professionally organized.

—that the shop has an ASE-certified mechanic or equivalent for *each* area of service it offers; or that it agrees to obtain ASE certification within two testing periods.

—that the garage is overseen by a qualified supervisor.

—that the shop has sufficient garagekeepers' legal liability insurance.

—that employees are given up-to-date training on new automotive systems.

—that service reception personnel are trained to advise customers regarding repairs and service.

Before granting approval, AAA checks into the shop's reputation in the community by consulting a financial report on the shop, the Council of the Better Business Bureaus, the consumer protection agency, and, perhaps most importantly, by surveying past customers of the shop at random.

If neither of these signs are hanging from the door of a repair shop you're thinking of patronizing, ask the owner if he's received either ASE-certification or AAA approval. While *not* belonging to either of these groups doesn't mean that a shop is unqualified, having these signs of competency should indicate to you that at least the shop is doing more than just the minimum to be in business repairing cars.

THE RIGHT WAY TO TALK TO A MECHANIC

Theoretically, if your mechanic is honest and trustworthy, it shouldn't matter *how* you approach him; he should do the best job he can without any hesitation. However, the hard truth is that if a mechanic, service manager, shop owner—or anyone with whom you deal directly in seeking service—identifies you as a "know-nothing pushover" you may be more likely to get poorer service at a higher price than someone who appears knowledgeable and confident.

Here are some suggestions for dealing with a mechanic.

BEFORE YOU GO INTO THE SHOP:
☐ Gain a basic understanding of how your car works, which you can get from reading this book.

☐ Write down any symptoms of a problem as you notice them. (This is one reason why it's helpful to keep a notepad and pen in your glove compartment at all times.) Try to be as specific as possible. Does the problem occur when the engine is cold, hot, warming up? Is the problem constant, or intermittent? Does it occur only in certain weather conditions? Only when you're driving at certain speeds? Only when you're making a turn? Braking? Accelerating? Using a particular accessory? The more specific you can be about the symptoms of a problem, the more accurately and quickly the mechanic will be able to narrow down the diagnosis and possible solutions.

☐ Bring in the car to a repair shop at a time when you won't be rushed, so you can explain the problem clearly to the mechanic and go for a test drive *with* the mechanic if necessary.

FACE-TO-FACE WITH THE MECHANIC:

☐ In explaining your car's problem, *don't* tell the mechanic what to do. There's a subtle difference between showing the mechanic you know what you're talking about, and trying to take over his job. If you go into a shop and say "my car's been stalling a lot; I think it needs a full tune-up," the mechanic may very well grant your wish—even if all it *really* needs is a slight, inexpensive adjustment to the choke. Such a mistake could be costly.

☐ Show the mechanic your list of specifics about your car's problem, so there's nothing you forget to tell him.

☐ Ask the mechanic to go on a test drive with you if there's something you can't quite articulate and prefer to demonstrate.

☐ Ask what the mechanic suspects the problem might be— and beware if the reply is a general, sweeping statement. If, without even looking under your hood, the mechanic says, "I think you need a new transmission" or "I'd suggest a complete engine overhaul," get a second opinion from another repair shop.

☐ Get a second opinion before proceeding with any major repair. Asking another mechanic only for a diagnosis might cost $50 or $60; but it could be worth it in the long run if he pinpoints a smaller problem, whereas another mechanic might suggest an "overhaul" of the car to cover many possibilities.

☐ Get an estimate in writing before the repair is performed. (This is a law in some states, but only if you request it.) Tell the mechanic that if the repair is going to cost more than the estimate suggests, you want to be notified *before* it's done; this will give you time to get a second opinion.

☐ Give the mechanic a phone number where you can be reached for further consultation if necessary.

☐ Ask the mechanic if you have a choice between new, remanufactured, and used replacement parts. While new parts generally carry the longest warranty (important if you plan to keep your car for many more years), remanufactured parts are much less expensive and virtually as good as new. They usually carry at least a one-year warranty (a good choice for older cars). Unless your car is very old, or you simply can't afford a remanufactured part, you should avoid used parts. They usually come with no warranty, and no one's exactly sure of their history. Always ask for a warranty on new and remanufactured parts.

☐ Trust your instincts about how you feel a repair shop will handle your car. Do you *feel* comfortable leaving your car with this mechanic? Is he or she willing to answer your questions without hesitation, and without being patronizing or condescending? If any of your answers are "no," don't feel you have to leave your car there. You're paying for a service and you have a right to turn and walk away if you're not getting what you want.

AFTER A REPAIR IS MADE:
☐ Always ask to see the old automobile part that was replaced. (Sometimes the shop needs to send the old part back to the manufacturer for warranty work so you may not be able to keep it.) Ask the mechanic to explain to you what was the problem with the old part. This can help you to understand what took place during the repair so you know what you're paying for. (While it's true that, technically, a mechanic could substitute another old auto part and pretend it's yours, most reliable shops won't do that.)

☐ Examine the repair bill thoroughly and ask questions if you don't understand something.

□ Make sure a copy of the repair warranty is on the bill; if it isn't, ask for the warranty in writing.

□ Go for a test drive right from the shop, *before* you pay the bill. If the car is still not running right, don't take it home; describe to the mechanic the problem you're still observing. If the car *is* running smoothly, let the mechanic know that you're pleased.

□ Keep a file of all your repair receipts, and any service records you have for your car. They'll come in handy if the same problem creeps up again later. They'll also be proof of your conscientious car ownership when it comes time to sell (or trade in) your car at a later point.

□ If you like an automobile repair shop, patronize it, and recommend it to your friends. The more business you give to a particular shop, the more respect and attention that shop owner and/or mechanic is likely to give you. His or her respect is an important commodity in these busy times when repairs are likely to be needed as soon as possible and when you want them done correctly the first time. Knowing a mechanic you can trust is one of the most comforting and valuable relationships you can establish. It could mean a longer life for your car, and safer traveling for you and your passengers.

5
Safe Driving All Year-round

Ideally, car owners would like to be able to drive on sunny days that aren't too hot or too cold, limit their driving to the daytime, and drive on smooth, pothole-free roads—all without worrying about any damage that could arise in their cars along the way.

The reality is, of course, that from time to time every driver has to travel in less-than-ideal conditions. Rain, snow, hot weather, and freezing temperatures can pose real challenges to your car—and to you as a driver. But there are ways to emerge from even the worst weather conditions unscathed. They begin with knowing how to adjust your driving strategies to meet the changing conditions that confront you. This chapter will show you how.

RAINY WEATHER DRIVING

As a driver and/or car owner, you should be aware that certain features of a car—such as disc brakes and radial tires—are better able to handle rainy weather than others.

Most cars manufactured today have disc brakes on the front wheels, drum brakes on the back; and more expensive cars often have disc brakes on all four wheels. Disc brakes are better able to handle wet weather than drum brakes because they dry out very quickly if they get wet. Brakes will not work efficiently if wet.

Radial tires seem to move through puddles better than other tires (particularly better than snow tires) because their tread designs often squeegee the water out from between the tire and the road. Some radials are better in the rain than others, so consult an independent tire dealer for recommendations for your kind of car and driving.

Precautions Before Driving

Before heading out for a drive when the forecast calls for "heavy rains," follow this list of helpful hints.

☐ Check windshield wipers. They're vitally important to your clear visibility. Make sure they sweep away rain without smearing it across your windshield. It's a good idea to keep a spare set in your trunk, too, in case they wear out while you're on a long trip on the road.

☐ Make sure headlights, turn signals, and brake lights are clean and in working order. Even in midday, a rainstorm can darken skies enough that it's wise to turn on your low beams so you can see more easily, but without adding so much light that the rain's reflection forms a glare. Your turn signals and brake lights are especially important in wet weather as warning signs to other drivers when you need to stop or to switch lanes.

☐ Check your front (and rear, if you have one) defroster. If you're heading out in a rainstorm, it's wise to sit in your car for two minutes or so and run the defrosters until your windows are completely clear. Your visibility will be limited enough without trying to see through steamy glass, too.

Driving Strategies

☐ Your car can be one of the safest forms of shelter if you're caught in the midst of a thunder/lightning storm. If lightning does strike your car, it will follow the metal contour of the body and "fall off" at the tires, leaving you and any passengers safe and unharmed. In most rainstorms, the "eye" of the storm will take only a few minutes to pass over you. Therefore, the most sensible thing to do in the center of a full-blown storm is to *pull over on the side of the road*—highway rest stops are especially good—*and just wait for the storm to subside.*

☐ Be alert to the possible unpredictable reactions of other drivers in rainy weather. Are they slamming on their brakes? Switching lanes recklessly to avoid puddles and potholes? Slowing down? Be ready to switch into lanes with less traffic, brake, or pull off the road suddenly, if necessary. Turn off the radio and any other distractions that could take your attention off the road. Be alert for any changes in road signs or conditions ahead.

☐ Slow down when approaching a bridge or overpass in rainy weather so you don't skid. In freezing weather (common in early spring or fall) rain will freeze more readily on bridges and can form icy, slick patches, conducive to skids.

☐ Slow down to drive within your limits of visibility. You will probably have to brake suddenly at least once in a rainstorm and the slower you're driving, the more quickly you'll be able to stop.

☐ If your brakes are completely gone—too wet to stop your car—gradually ease over onto the side of the road and stop at the most convenient place possible. Never continue driving a car without working brakes.

☐ Drive through deep puddles slowly to avoid soaking your engine parts with water that sprays up inside. Wet spark plugs, wires, coil, and distributor could cause your car to stall—and it won't start again until all those parts dry out. (Sometimes you can facilitate this process by drying any visible parts yourself with a towel. However, it's impractical to lift your hood to dry these parts unless you're under an overpass or some sort of covering; otherwise, you might let more rain inside.)

☐ Try to anticipate—and avoid—hydroplaning. It's the situation that occurs sometimes if you drive too fast through a puddle—or even over a road covered evenly with a quarter inch or so of water. If you're driving 30 m.p.h. or more, your front wheels (especially if the tread is worn) can sometimes "lift" off the road and ride buoyantly on the surface of the water like a surfboard. (Hence the term "hydro"—meaning water, "plane"—meaning surface.) This "lifting" can cause your back wheels to skid or cause you to lose brake and/or steering control. It is equivalent to being on ice.

To avoid hydroplaning, try to drive around puddles; if you have to go through them, slow down ahead of time, but don't brake going through them. Deep puddles are not the hazard that shallow patches of water on the road are.

Make sure your tires are properly inflated and the treads are deep; the deeper the treads, the more water they will take up and the less chance that they'll ride up on the water's surface.

In traffic, try to drive in the "tracks" of the wheels of the car in front of you. There will be less water in these tracks than alongside them, so there will be less chance that your tires will ride up on the water. The slower your speed, the more time your tires have to disperse water between the tread and the road.

☐ After you drive through a deep puddle (where the water reaches over the tires to the wheels), lightly pump your brake pedal to create heat, drying out the brakes' friction surfaces.

HOT WEATHER HAZARDS

An automobile engine can reach temperatures up to 5,000° F. under normal operating circumstances. Compound this with high outside temperatures and you can see how summer heat can be a big challenge for your car.

Your engine can overheat in any kind of weather due to a variety of reasons—a heavier-than-usual load (e.g., towing a trailer), a radiator coolant or oil leak, or thermostat malfunction. However, it's more likely to overheat on a steamy summer day than in cold weather since (1) your engine is simply operating at a slightly higher temperature; and (2) you're more likely to be running the air conditioner, which greatly taxes the radiator's cooling capacity.

So, on hot summer days, stay alert to your car's temperature gauge or warning light and turn off these engine-stressing accessories *before* the needle rises up to the danger zone on your temperature gauge. If the temperature gauge does register in the danger zone, you can alternate between riding with the windows open and riding with your air conditioner on for a while, or turn off engine-stressing accessories altogether, at least until you can pull safely into a service station to look for the problem.

What to Do If Your Car Overheats

1) First, turn off the air conditioner.
2) Try not to follow cars too closely in stop-and-go traffic. You'll end up sucking up some of the heated exhaust from the car in front of you, further stressing your car's cooling system.
3) If you're caught in stop-and-go traffic, put your car in neutral when you've stopped. While in neutral, gently press the accelerator to raise your engine idle speed; this will increase the coolant flow through your engine and the radiator.
4) If, after taking the above steps, your temperature gauge still reads in the danger zone, turn on your car heater and blower; they will pull the heat away from your engine parts into the car interior. The few minutes of sweltering that you have to endure could save your engine and enable you to drive off safely in the end; it's worth it.
5) If these measures don't cause your temperature gauge to read lower, pull off the road immediately and stop the car. The longer you drive with an overheating engine, the more damage you'll cause to individual engine parts.

Finding the Cause of a Car's Overheating

1) Make sure the car's engine is cool before you begin to look for the problem.

2) Look to see if your car has blown a hose or broken a belt. If so, and you don't have an extra belt or hose in your trunk, don't attempt to drive the car any further. Call for someone to tow your car to a service station.

3) If all hoses and belts look all right, check your car's oil level. One of oil's many roles in the operation of your car is that of cooling engine parts. Therefore, a low oil level (caused either by negligence in checking the level, or an oil leak) could cause an engine to overheat rapidly. *If lack of oil is the problem,* add some, if you have a spare quart in your trunk. If you don't have a quart of oil, try to call a service station or wait for someone to stop and help you. *If you suspect an oil leak,* get your car to a service station as soon as possible. Never drive if your car is lacking oil; you could cause serious damage to engine parts in seconds.

4) If your oil level is all right, check your car's radiator coolant level by looking in the reservoir tank. If the tank is empty, there's a good chance that lack of radiator coolant is the problem. However, even if the coolant level in the reservoir is high, lack of coolant could still be your problem: your pressure cap could be faulty, thus not sealing the pressure in the radiator to resist coolant boiling, or your thermostat could be malfunctioning.

To check the coolant level in the radiator itself, put on gloves or at least use a towel or thick rag to protect your hand, and gently loosen the radiator pressure cap just slightly; then step back. Never use your bare hand on the radiator cap of a hot engine. Allow the steam and hot water to escape and lessen the pressure in the radiator itself. After a few minutes, remove the pressure cap completely and look into the radiator. If you see no signs of the greenish antifreeze, you need to add some (see instructions, p. 27). Fill up the radiator with coolant, then start the car's engine and let it idle for a few minutes to let the coolant circulate. Add more as the coolant begins to circulate and fill up the reservoir tank.

5) Check the condition of the radiator cap. Is the rubber around it deteriorating so that the seal it creates on your radiator is not airtight? A faulty radiator cap is a common reason why a car overheats; it's not allowing enough pressure to build inside the radiator to raise the boiling temperature of the coolant to the optimum level. If this is the case, once you've refilled the radiator with coolant, drive only to the nearest service station and have the radiator cap replaced.

6) If none of these readily apparent signs of overheating are present, your problem could be more subtle. Are you towing an unusually heavy load? If so, your car is probably simply not equipped to handle such weight.

If your car is not towing an unusually heavy load, the problem is probably deeper within your engine—a malfunction in your ignition system, a faulty radiator or thermostat, or any number of problems. The best thing to do is to call a tow truck to take your car to a repair shop.

What to Do If Smoke Comes Out of Your Car's Hood

1) Pull off the road immediately and stop the car.

2) Turn the engine completely off and wait at least thirty minutes for it to cool before looking for the problem.

3) Carefully raise your car's hood and step back from the engine to avoid possibly being burned by any hot spewing liquids.

4) It's unlikely that common overheating will lead to a fire. However, if you do see flames under your car's hood, use a fire extinguisher or sand to put it out. *Never* spray water on a burning engine, because if there's an oil or gas leak the water will cause these flammable fluids to spread to other parts of your engine.

DRIVING TIPS IN AUTUMN

Autumn may be one of the prettiest times of the year, but when those multicolored leaves drop off the trees, they can present some pretty tricky situations for you as a driver and car owner. Here are a few suggestions to keep in mind.

□ On cold autumn days, an icy road is twice as slippery when the temperature is just at freezing as when it's much below that. Drive more slowly and be prepared to brake slowly in this kind of "transitional" weather.

□ Never park your car over a pile of leaves (no matter how small the pile). During driving, your catalytic converter (located underneath your car) builds up considerable heat and it takes several minutes after you've parked to cool down. During that time, your catalytic converter *could* ignite the leaves below it, causing considerable damage.

□ Try not to park under a tree whose leaves are dropping. Tree sap (a little drop of which is found at the end of almost every fallen leaf) is one of the trickiest things to remove from a car, and it can eat away your car's body paint.

SNOWY WEATHER DRIVING

If you are a knowledgeable car owner, your car should be well braced to face the threats of cold-weather winter, heavy snow falls, hidden patches of ice, cold morning temperatures that put stress on your battery—to name just a few. No matter how cautious you are, often you can't avoid these situations completely, so it's worth thinking ahead of time how to handle the special challenges of snowy weather driving.

Trunk Checklist

□ The year-round equipment mentioned in chapter one (including jumper cables, jack and spare tire, blanket, first aid kit, extra antifreeze, windshield washer fluid, oil, emergency flares, etc.).

□ A good, square-bladed snow shovel.

☐ Wire traction mats, or old pieces of carpeting, for help in pulling out of an icy parking spot.

☐ A bag of kitty litter, rock salt, or *dry* sand (wet sand will freeze and be useless) to provide extra traction on ice or in snowy parking spots.

☐ Combination ice scraper and snow brush for cleaning off windshields and car body.

NOTE: Also, have on hand a small aerosol container of lock de-icer, available from your local hardware store; but *don't keep this in your trunk or glove compartment.* If your locks are frozen, you'll probably need it to get into your car or trunk.

Servicing Your Car

While there's never a bad time to have a tune-up, right before winter sets in might be one of the better times. Since cars have a tougher time starting on a cold morning than just about any other time of year, at least make sure that your new spark plugs will give your automobile a fighting chance to start right up on a frosty morning. Whether or not you have a full tune-up, you should have your car serviced before winter, making sure that the mechanic does the following:

—changes the oil, if necessary, to a lighter viscosity that's better able to handle cold weather.

—tests the battery, alternator, and voltage regulator to ensure that they're charging well and that all connections are tight and not corroded.

—checks the antifreeze, and flushes the radiator with new antifreeze, if it's two years old.

—uses a waterproofing solution on all exposed ignition wires.

—examines the exhaust system and muffler for possible leaks.

—checks the brakes and examines the fluid level in the master cylinder.

—checks the heater, defroster, and all lights to make sure they're working well.

—changes the regular windshield wipers for snow blades if necessary; these wipers usually have a rubber "hood" that prevents snow from sticking to the wiping part of the blade.

When to Use Snow Tires

Today there are more choices in tire types than ever before, and some tires are able to handle so many different kinds of situations that in some cases, they can eliminate the necessity for changing over to snow tires in the wintertime. Of course, this depends on where you live and what kind of car you drive.

In some areas (the mountainous regions of California, for example) snow tires are not enough. Tire chains are needed on some roads at specified times. Other areas forbid the use of studded tires because they tend to cut up the roads they travel on.

Front-wheel drive automobiles automatically offer better straight-ahead traction in snow than rear-wheel drive cars, so that feature could also reduce the need for snow tires. If your car currently has "all-season" tires, and you don't get a great amount of snowfall in the area in which you live, those tires—while they won't provide you as good traction in snow as snow tires—may be just enough to get you through the winter, provided their treads are in good shape.

Also, if your main concern is ice—and not snow—you may be better off with regular tires than some snow tires. Tests conducted by the National Safety Council revealed that some regular tires offered greater braking traction on ice than some ordinary snow tires (not studded tires or those covered by snow chains), while snow tires inevitably offer better braking on snow.

If you do want to put snow tires on your car this winter, here are some tips.

□ Have snow tires put on when the temperature drops, but before the first snowfall. Since snow tires require your engine to burn slightly more fuel because they have more rolling resistance than normal tires, you don't want to put them on too early, or leave them on too long in the springtime.

□   Store your regular tires in an enclosed, dry place. Lay them flat, as opposed to standing them up (which would put all the weight of the tire on one spot, wearing it out early, and potentially causing the rest of your tire to become flabby). Make sure they're fully inflated before storing them.

□   *Don't* underinflate your snow tires. It's a common myth that underinflating your tires, even slightly, will provide better traction in snow. What it *will* do is make the car handle poorly, cause the tires to wear out faster, and make them more likely to blow out on the highway.

□   Don't load up your trunk excessively, thinking that the extra weight will give better traction in snow. If you have a front-wheel drive car, extra weight in the trunk will, in fact, worsen traction.

Getting a Clear Start

□   On a snowy morning, give yourself extra time to clean off your car thoroughly before you head out on the road. If you clear off only your windows and windshield, and leave a pile of snow on the roof of your car, that snow can blow off during driving and hamper your visibility.

□   Clear off your driver's door first; then get in the car. Start up the car, turning on the defroster. With the engine running, check to make sure that the exhaust is coming easily out of the exhaust pipe and that it's not clogged with snow, which could cause deadly carbon monoxide to seep into the interior of your car.

□   Brush off the remaining snow all around your car and gently scrape off the ice from your windows and windshield, although your defroster should begin to melt the snow from these areas.

☐ Make sure headlights and turn signals are clear and working.

☐ Get into the car every few minutes and depress the accelerator pedal partway to keep the engine's idle speed from becoming too fast.

Getting the Feel of the Road

☐ Before you head out on any busy roads on a cold snowy day, it's a good idea first to test out the weather conditions on a less-traveled (but plowed) road. Accelerate gently to see if your wheels are likely to spin and apply varying pressures to your brakes to see how quickly you can brake before your wheels "lock up" (stop turning).

☐ Once you have a general feel for how you should adjust your driving to the outside weather conditions, you can head out on the highway with a better idea of how to space yourself from other cars. Allow more following (and hence, braking) distance on snowy or icy roads than on clear ones. These road conditions also require you to be alert to the changing intentions of other drivers—to their turn signals and brake lights— and modify your driving behavior accordingly.

How to Brake on an Icy Surface

There's a right and wrong way to brake on icy, slick surfaces. The *right way* is to apply pressure on the brake pedal slowly and easily, "squeezing" the brake pedal gently rather than giving it one great jolt. The *wrong way* is to slam on your brakes, or to "pump" your brakes (moving your foot up and down on the pedal). These methods will cause your wheels to lock up, sending your car into a skid.

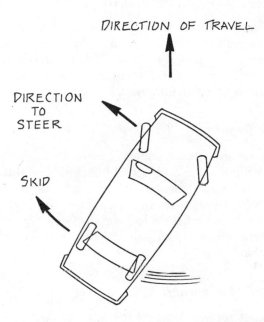

DIRECTION OF TRAVEL

DIRECTION
TO
STEER

SKID

**In case of skid, steer in the direction
the rear of the car is sliding.**

How to Get Out of a Skid

1) Turn your steering wheel *slightly* (never make sweeping turns when you're skidding) so your car's wheels point in the direction you want to go.

2) Hold the steering wheel firmly; *ease off* the accelerator, and *stay off* the brake. It also helps to put the gear shift in "neutral." Your first instinct when your car goes out of control in a skid is to slam on the brakes, but this will worsen the skid.

3) Once you feel the car straighten out, turn the wheel straight and keep rolling.

Since it takes a few experiences with skids to get skilled at steering out of them, it may be a good idea, at the first sign of icy weather, to drive your car to a big, empty, icy parking lot and practice getting your car in and out of skids. After doing it a few times, you're bound to get the feel for the right action to take, and you won't panic when it happens for real when you're driving down the highway.

Parking Problems

During, or just after, a snowfall, before you park your car anywhere, think of the ease with which you'll be able to pull it out again. Whenever possible, it's best to avoid parallel parking, as it's hard to get out of a parking space if you have to turn your steering wheel a lot. Besides, you won't have the added worry of potentially damaging the cars parked in front of and behind you.

How to Get Unstuck

1) If there's snow around your car, first check your exhaust pipe to make sure it's not clogged with snow; if it is, use a stick or other long thin object to clear away the snow.
2) Start up your car and while it's warming, move your steering wheel from side to side so that your tires clear away the snow immediately around them.
3) To get moving, apply very light pressure to the accelerator. (Sometimes it helps to keep one foot lightly on the brake pedal to ensure that you don't accelerate too fast.)
4) Once you feel the car move forward, continue to apply slow, steady pressure on the accelerator and steer straight ahead, if possible. *Do not* push down hard on the accelerator to get the car moving, as this could cause your wheels to dig two icy trenches in the snow, from which it will be even harder to exit.
5) If your wheels spin in their tracks, take your foot off the accelerator. If you continue to accelerate, your wheels will dig trenches deeper and deeper in the snow. Get out of the car, and either pour kitty litter, sand, or rock salt around your tires to give them some traction, or use traction mats or old pieces of

carpeting. Get back in your car and, once again, apply slow, steady pressure to the accelerator.

6) If adding this traction doesn't help, you may want to try "rocking" the car; but before you do this, consult your owner's manual. Sometimes rocking the car can cause transmission damage. If your owner's manual doesn't advise against rocking, here's how you do it:

—with someone standing behind your car, apply slight pressure to the accelerator, as the person pushes the car from behind (or from the side of the car, if that's easier and safer).

—if the car doesn't lift out of the trench right away, ease up on the accelerator and let the car drop back a bit (but not all the way) before you apply slight pressure on the accelerator again, while being pushed by your assistant.

—continue this back and forth movement until the car gains enough momentum to pull itself (with the help from the accelerator and the person pushing) out of the icy grooves and on its way.

TIPS FOR LONG-DISTANCE DRIVING

More and more people these days are deciding to vacation by car—a trend that's due, in part, to today's more fuel-efficient automobiles, and in part to the enjoyment of seeing firsthand the scenic beauty of the country. Before you set out on some extended pleasure driving, however, there are some ways to prepare ahead of time to ensure that your vacation will be safe—and in terms of on-the-road problems—happily uneventful.

BEFORE YOU HEAD OUT:

☐ Have your car professionally serviced before you set out on the highway. If you plan far enough ahead, have a full tune-up done on your car. If your car is not due for a full tune-up, at least have your mechanic check the condition of your brakes, tires, radiator, and oil to make sure that they're all in good shape.

☐ Run through your "weekly" maintenance checklist (see pp. 186–87), paying special attention to your car's turn signals, headlights and taillights, windshield wipers and washer fluid, and tire inflation, as well as brake performance, shock absorbers, and the condition of all your car's belts and hoses.

☐ Review your driving plans and know your physical limits. Some people can drive ten hours comfortably with brief rest stops; others are exhausted after five hours. Never push yourself beyond your capabilities since your driving—and consequently the safety of you and your passengers—is sure to suffer. Stop for coffee breaks at least every two hours, and when possible, share the driving with a passenger. Try to predict when you might get into traffic and plan to set out on your trip either before or after those times (for instance, before or after the morning commuter rush hour).

☐ Limit the number of distractions in the car. On a hot summer day, with your windows rolled up, the air conditioner on, and your radio blaring at top decibels, it can be impossible to hear the warning sounds of the vehicles around you—whether the horn of a passing motorist or the sirens of an emergency vehicle. Keep your radio volume low, and, especially if you use air conditioning, be alert to the intentions of cars around you and changes in the road.

☐ Each night before you set out the next morning, take some time to study your maps to plot out the driving course you're going to take the next day. It's extremely dangerous to try to read maps while you're driving on the highway. Removing your eyes from the road for even a moment could cause you to swerve off the road or into another lane, or make you oblivious to the actions of other drivers. If you need to double-check your route while on the road, pull off at a highway rest stop, an exit, or if necessary, onto the breakdown lane or highway shoulder.

☐ During your trip, give your car a five-minute checkup every morning before you head out on the highway, including headlights, brake lights, and directionals to make sure they're working well and are clean; tire inflation and condition—pull out any obvious foreign objects in treads like glass or nails that could embed themselves and cause an air leak on the highway; oil, coolant, windshield washer fluid and, of course, gasoline levels; and be sure to adjust side- and rearview mirrors.

☐ Have your car well equipped for a trip. In addition to the gear you should always have in your trunk and glove compartment (see pp. 2–4), stock your glove compartment with detailed maps of your destinations, and a travel log in which you can write down gas mileage and car maintenance costs on your trip, as well as any suspicious sounds, smells, or performance changes in your car you can report to your mechanic when you get home. A long trip is a good time to take stock of the overall performance of your car, and to notice things that you both like and dislike about the car's performance. All these observations will come in handy when you're ready to trade in your current model and buy a new car. And the travel log will act as a great memento of your trip, as well as an aid in planning your next driving vacation.

ON-THE-ROAD DRIVING TECHNIQUES:

☐ Keep alert and avoid the greatest hazard of a long drive, namely "driver's trance." You'll often hear people say that they can't remember where they drove during the last half hour. To a certain extent, driver's trance is a natural consequence of gaining the "feel" of the road and falling into a nice driving rhythm with other cars around you; it's the exact opposite of the person who drives on the edge of his seat, convinced that at any moment he or she is going to be sideswiped by a careless driver and always ready to slam on the brakes.

As soon as you realize that you're not as alert or paying as much attention to other drivers and road conditions as you should, it's time to pull off the road for a break, even just a few minutes to get out of your car and stretch. Just those few minutes can refresh you enough for another hour of more alert, less oblivious driving.

To avoid driver's trance, keep a window slightly open at all times

—even if you have the heater or air conditioner on—to keep fresh air constantly flowing into the car. Eat lightly the night before and on refreshment stops; a heavy meal can make you feel sluggish and sleepy at the wheel. Never drink alcohol and drive, as even one drink containing alcohol can make you feel sleepy, throw off your reflexes, and make you less alert. Wear comfortable clothes. Listen to a lively radio station (at low volume so you can still hear sounds around you) but not a program that's so distracting that you stop paying attention to road signs and changes in road conditions. Sometimes it helps to choose a more "scenic" route over a direct, but boring, highway. Your attention will be maximized by the scenery around you.

□ Turn your headlights on at the first signs of the sky darkening—whether due to diminishing daylight or the onset of heavy rain, snow, or fog. Not only can headlights help you to see better, they help other cars recognize that you're approaching so they can get out of your way.

□ Avoid glare from oncoming cars at night by driving in the right lane and keeping your vision on the edge lines of the highway. Never stare directly into the headlights of oncoming cars. If approaching cars' bright high-beam headlights are temporarily blinding you, flick your own headlights from low to high to signal the cars to turn down their lights.

□ Keep adequate space between you and other vehicles on the road. Ideally, the rule is to keep two "seconds" between you and the car in front of you when driving conditions are good. Watch as the car in front of you passes a particular landmark, such as a road sign; then begin counting (one thousand one; one thousand two). You should be able to say "two" before your car passes the same landmark. If you can't, slow down to widen the gap. When traffic is heavy, keeping this ideal spacing is not easy, but do your best. Four seconds of space is recommended in bad weather.

□ Make way for trucks. They're bigger and heavier than your

passenger car and they won't be able to slow down or to stop as readily as you can. If you have to pass a truck, always do so on the left; most truck drivers have a blind spot by the right side of their vehicle. Make the truck driver well aware of your intentions to pass by with your turn signals, and perhaps, giving your horn a friendly toot, and/or flashing your headlights quickly so they reflect in his sideview mirror.

Once past the truck, make sure you can see it easily in your rearview mirror before changing back into the right lane. There should be enough space between your car and the truck so that if you have to stop suddenly, the truck will have enough time to stop or change lanes.

When it's raining, switch your windshield wipers to high speed when driving beside a truck since the spray from its exposed tires can throw enough rain on your windshield to temporarily blind your vision. In windy weather, your car can swerve unpredictably when passing a truck since it can act as a wind block—until you pull away from it.

Whenever possible, try to stay well clear of trucks. In some areas, laws require trucks to drive only in certain lanes. If that's true where you are, you should avoid driving in those lanes. Never try to "outdo" a truck by not allowing it to pass you, or by trying to drive faster than it is.

TOWING A TRAILER OR CAMPER

Camping is becoming an increasingly popular way to travel around the country, owing in part to the rising costs of airfare and hotel rooms, but also to the fact that it provides an opportunity in this ever-urbanized society to appreciate the outdoors, while still enjoying many of the comforts of home. Towing a trailer and/or camper is a simple and rewarding experience, once you "get the hang of it." But there's a lot you should know before attempting to add the extra weight of a trailer or camper to your car. Even if you never go on a camping trip, chances are that someday you'll be carrying a heavier-than-usual load—whether you're packing up your daughter for a semester in college and you have to rent a weekend trailer, or you're moving to a new location on your own. Make sure you know what you're doing *before* you set out on the road.

Before you spend a single dollar to rent or buy a trailer, read your automobile owner's manual to ensure that your car is capable of *towing* a trailer. (Many of today's compact cars are not.) Towing a trailer puts extremely heavy stress on your braking system, suspension system, tires, and engine. It's not worth the risk of damage to your car to try to tow that extra

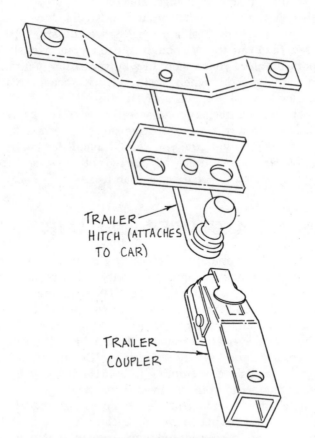

Weight-carrying hitch

weight if your automobile isn't adequately equipped to do so. Know the vehicle load limits of your car and of any trailer that you're thinking of towing, specified by manufacturer's recommendations.

Once you've decided on a trailer that your car can safely tow, make sure to get the right kind of hitch to hook it up correctly; different size and weight trailers require different kinds of hitches.

Weight-carrying hitches are used for towing lightweight (2,000 pounds or less) trailers *only*. The rear end of your car will support the hitch weight of the trailer and simply will not be able to handle any heavier loads.

Weight-distribution (load-equalizer) *hitches* are designed to distribute the trailer's total weight evenly between your car's

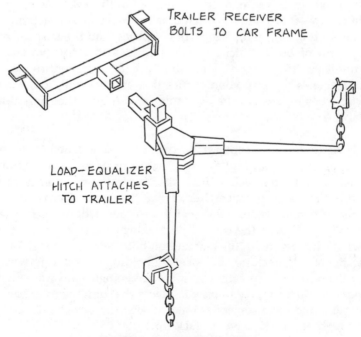

Weight-distribution hitch

front and rear wheels and the trailer wheels; some also incorporate an antisway device to prevent the trailer from swinging from side to side as you're driving and, thus, provide you with more control.

Towing Safety

Your driving strategy requires some revision when you've got many hundreds of extra pounds to account for on the road. Towing a trailer changes your limits of visibility, alters your ability to pass, to accelerate, to change lanes, to merge, to pull off the highway—in short, you, as a driver, need to rethink almost every move you make on the road when your car is towing a trailer. Here are some suggestions to help ensure a safe and happy trailering trip for you and your passengers.

BEFORE YOU HEAD OUT ON THE HIGHWAY:

☐ Have your car and the trailer—and the security of the hitch-up—thoroughly inspected, with special attention paid to shock absorbers and springs, brakes, tires, and the suspension systems of both vehicles. It's a good idea to carry two spare tires if you're going on a long trip, since if one trailer tire blows out, there's a pretty good chance that another will, too. Keep your tires inflated to the maximum pressure on their inflation label (see p. 69).

☐ After their inspection, take your car and attached trailer to a large empty parking lot and practice turns and backing up; there's a certain knack to driving with a trailer that comes only with time and practice. Remember that you need a much greater turning radius, and that your trailer will move further right or left than the car will in making a turn. Keep alert to what's happening in the rear and on both sides of your car and trailer as you back up, and steer by holding the steering wheel at the bottom for greater control when going backward. When possible on a trip, try to park in places that don't require backing up, and have someone stand outside the vehicle, directing you, when you *do* have to back up.

☐ Equip your car with large (trucklike) temporary rearview mirrors on both driver's and passenger's sides to allow better visibility of oncoming cars on either side of the trailer. Use these mirrors often while driving.

☐ When loading the trailer, it's vitally important to keep balance in mind. Never overload either the trailer or your car. If the trailer sags to one side or another, shift the load to attain a level side-to-side "attitude." (The "attitude" means the levelness of the car and trailer; neither the trailer nor the towing vehicle should lean too much to the right or left, or weigh down too heavily in the front or back.) Load heavy items low and near the center of the trailer, preferably over or just in front of the axle; never load heavy items in upper cabinets. Make sure that all items are securely fastened in place so that they don't shift during travel.

☐ Load all emergency gear, tools, and an electric extension cord with a light in a convenient, readily accessible location; your car trunk is probably the best spot. If your trailer holds a water tank, load and weigh the trailer with the tank full, and as the tank empties throughout the trip, adjust the rest of the load accordingly to account for the weight change.

☐ Before you head out on a trip, bring your trailer and car to a weighing station that has platform scales (such as building supply companies, moving and storage companies, some junkyards). Weigh the loaded trailer alone to make sure that it does not exceed the manufacturer's Gross Vehicle Weight Rating (GVWR)—the maximum load for which the trailer is designed. If it does, you'll have to remove some of the heavier dispensable items and keep weighing the trailer until it meets the GVWR. When the total trailer weight is okay, weigh the trailer with just the hitch resting on the scale. The weight measured this way should be about 10 percent of the total trailer weight for safe balance and towing. Finally, make sure the hitch-up to your car follows all the requirements outlined in your car's owner's manual.

ON THE ROAD:

☐ As a rule, drive slower than you would as a single passenger car. In some states, trailer-towing vehicles are required by law to drive slower than passenger cars and a different speed for them is specified. If you're going to be driving through different states, it would be wise before heading out on your trip to check out the motor vehicle laws in each state to avoid driving too far over the speed limit.

☐ Avoid abrupt braking that could cause your trailer to jack-knife (a situation in which the trailer's back wheels spring up in the air). Since it will take longer for your car to come to a complete stop because you're pulling so much extra weight, make sure to allow plenty of space between your car and the cars in front of you.

☐ Never let any passenger stay in the trailer while you're moving, as this will cause a shift in trailer weight balance that could endanger both the trailer-riding passenger, as well as the passengers and driver in your trailer-towing car.

☐ When changing lanes, or making turns, avoid abrupt turns of the steering wheel. Gradually pull out and around the car you're passing, and return to your original lane just as slowly and deliberately, making very sure all is clear before you reenter the lane. Check your front and side mirrors carefully at all times.

☐ When driving over bumpy or wet roads, go even slower than your normal speed. Going over bumps quickly could cause your hitch to scrape and become damaged; and wet roads further inhibit your ability to stop when you need to.

☐ If you're driving in mountainous areas, be sure to carry extra radiator coolant since overheating is more likely in high altitudes.

☐ When driving up or down steep hills, shift to a lower gear. If your car has automatic transmission, it will shift automatically when you're driving uphill to give the car more traction. When going downhill, all cars, whether equipped with automatic or manual transmission, need to be shifted to a lower gear manually, to give better control to the towing vehicle.

☐ At least once a day during a trip, do a ten-minute maintenance check of both your car and your trailer. Pay special attention to tire inflation, making sure to check them only after several hours of nondriving (preferably first thing in the morning). Trailer tires usually need more air pressure than car tires do. During the trip, examine tires for bulging and excessive wear since heat build-up with such heavy vehicles can be extensive.

WHAT TO DO IF YOU'RE IN AN ACCIDENT

Until you're immersed in the middle of it, there's no way to predict exactly how you're going to behave in a crisis. Emergencies, by definition, happen at the most unexpected times, and there's no way to brace yourself right before they occur. But there are ways to think and prepare far ahead of time for the more technical things you should do in case an emergency situation occurs.

☐ Choose a car that has good safety features. Some of the things to look for are: front and rear seatbelts and shoulder straps (make sure that you and all passengers use them); air bags; a padded, well-illuminated dashboard with recessed knobs; adjustable headrests and mirrors; anti-lacerative windshields; and antilock brakes.

☐ Check your car quickly every time before you drive. Are the mirrors adjusted? Are the tires inflated correctly? Are the headlights clean? Do the windshield wipers work well? Thinking ahead is all part of being the best driver you can be—and that means improved safety for you and every other car on the road.

☐ Make sure your insurance is up-to-date and that your insurance card is readily accessible—either in your glove compartment or a wallet that you carry everywhere.

☐ Have a well-equipped glove compartment and trunk (see pp. 2–4).

☐ Take pictures of your car in perfect condition and have them on file with other information about your car; they may be helpful later on in a court case, or just to help with repairs.

☐ Check with your motor vehicle department for the amount of combined damage that can be done to two cars in an accident before the accident *must* be reported to the police. (This amount can vary from $50 to $500 from state to state.)

IF YOUR CAR HITS ANOTHER CAR OR PEDESTRIAN:
☐ If there is serious injury to a pedestrian or passenger, leave the car(s) in place. If there is not serious injury, move the car(s) to an emergency lane, parking lot, or out of traffic's way. A minor accident can become a major accident in a matter of seconds if there's a "chain reaction"—car upon car colliding to avoid hitting the two cars involved in the initial accident.

☐ Check for any serious injuries to passengers and drivers. Perform first aid *only* if you know how. Try to get to a phone to call an ambulance, or wave down a passing motorist to call for you.

☐ Whether or not you move the cars off the road, make them clearly visible to passing motorists by setting up flares or reflectors. Turn on your car's emergency flashers. If you need to direct oncoming traffic, do it from the side of the road, not in the middle.

☐ Once you know that everybody is all right, begin exchanging information with the other people involved in the accident. The information you exchange should include:

—drivers' licenses and license plate numbers.

—the year and make of the cars involved.

—names, addresses, and telephone numbers of drivers, passengers, and any available witnesses.

—if the driver of the other car is not the owner, the name, address, and phone number of the person to whom the car is registered.

—the name and address of the other driver's insurance company and agent (available on insurance cards).

—if police attend the accident, the officers' names and badge numbers, and the police precinct where the report is to be filed.

☐ Take detailed notes as soon as possible after the accident occurs. The weather conditions, road conditions, and the reactions of everybody involved in the accident should be included. Draw a diagram of the way the cars collided and write down, with as much detail as possible, the exact events of the accident as you remember them (but keep this information to yourself). The more you can remember right after the accident, the stronger your case will be when you file your insurance claim.

☐ Report the accident as soon as possible to the correct authorities. If the accident involves injury or death, or if the costs of damages in minor accidents exceed a certain amount designated by state law, you must call the police. *All* accidents must be reported to your state transportation or motor-vehicle department within a certain time limit set by your state law. (Ten days is common.) Accident report forms are available from transportation offices, local police, and your insurance agent.

☐ What *not* to do:

—*never* discuss the kind of insurance coverage you have with the other people involved in the accident.

—*never* try to reason with a hysterical or threatening person. Instead, try to separate yourself from them and look at the accident as objectively as possible.

—*never* admit guilt. Your perception might be off and you

might think you *are* guilty, or you may feel sorry for the other driver because he or she is very upset, and you want to take the blame to calm them down—but don't do it. Anything you say now could be used against you later on in court.

—*never* leave the scene of an accident unless you feel your safety is in danger; if you fail to stop after an accident or fail to cooperate with other rational drivers, you could lose your license or face criminal proceedings. If you feel the other people involved in the accident are threatening to your safety, don't try to reason with them; jot down their license plate number(s) and a description of the car(s) and leave. Immediately drive to a phone and call the police. If you explain to the police immediately why you left the scene of the accident, usually they won't press charges.

IF YOUR CAR HITS A PARKED CAR OR OTHER PRIVATE PROPERTY:

If you hit the fence around someone's home, or a tree on their front lawn, or a parked car with no one in it, or some other unclaimed private property, the best thing to do is to try to find the owners. If they are nowhere to be found, leave a note with your name, address, and telephone number. Write down their address or license plate number, and make and model of the car for your own records, and report the incident to the police.

IF YOUR CAR HITS PUBLIC PROPERTY:

If your car hits public property, such as a telephone pole or stop sign, call the police immediately. You are responsible for replacing the item. Your insurance should cover the costs.

IF YOUR CAR HITS AN ANIMAL:

If your car should hit an animal with a collar, see if you can find out the owner's name and telephone number to alert him. If you hit a wild animal—such as a deer—notify the police or the local department of conservation. Never try to pick up or aid a wild animal; if it is injured, it may try to bite or attack you and could cause you serious injury.

HOW TO PROTECT YOUR CAR FROM BEING STOLEN

There are few situations as upsetting as discovering that something has been stolen from your car or that the car itself has disappeared from the space where you parked it. Unfortunately, the number of drivers who endure this unpleasant experience is ever-increasing. Auto theft constitutes the biggest property crime in the United States today. Whether or not you're actually a victim of auto theft, you may pay for these statistics in your insurance.

Some car thieves are so "rehearsed" in their craft that they can pick a lock and electrically bypass the ignition switch in as little as forty seconds—less time than it may take you to start the engine with your key. These days, when and if cars are recovered, they've usually already fallen victim to "chop shops," illegal garages where stolen cars are dismantled into sections or individual parts that can be easily sold for a profit and used in other cars. Some car thefts involve disguising the car with a new paint job or other changes and reselling it. Still other cars that are reported stolen aren't really stolen at all, but are instruments of insurance fraud.

But, for most of us, the main concern is how to reduce your chances of being a victim of auto theft. First of all, you should be aware that luxury or sports cars have a theft rate as much as fifteen times greater than that of more conservative automobiles. Secondly, if you live in a high-crime urban area, your risk of auto theft goes up even more, and you may pay extra insurance for these added concerns. The majority of car thefts occur within a few miles of a car owner's home, often during a quick errand when he leaves the car running in order to dash into a store, only to find his car gone when he returns.

Though some drivers feel that car theft is an unfortunate "fate" for some people ("once thieves set their eyes on your car, there's nothing you can do to stop them"), law enforcement officers claim that *any* theft deterrent on your car will make a would-be thief less likely to attempt it; chances are, he'll move on to a less-difficult "job." Here are some good proven methods of reducing your chances of car theft.

Antitheft Devices

There's a reason why installing antitheft devices on your car entitles you to an insurance discount with some agencies: they work. Alarms, complicated locks, and cutoff switches all make your car that much more difficult to steal than an unprotected vehicle. Depending on what you can afford, you can buy anything from a $15 cutoff switch to a $600 switch/siren/flashing headlight system—and both would be effective in their own ways.

CUTOFF SWITCHES:

Cutoff switches come in two varieties: one will stop the flow of electricity to your ignition; the other will stop the flow of gasoline to your engine. Ignition cutoffs can be installed with a separate, extra switch on your ignition under the dashboard, or even behind the sun visor; and if a thief tries to bypass your normal ignition switch, the cutoff switch will prevent the car from starting. You can install an ignition cutoff yourself for as little as $15. Gasoline cutoffs ensure that a thief will be able to drive the car only a few blocks before it "runs out of gas." These devices must be installed by a mechanic and cost about $100.

ALARMS:

Think about the chaos a loud alarm can cause and you'll understand why they work so well. Most thieves will race off at the first sound of the siren. You can buy alarms that are triggered by the door, hood, or trunk switches. They come in a wide price range, depending on the sophistication of the system and the make of your car. (As with most accessories, the higher the original cost of your car, the higher the cost of installing antitheft devices.) All alarms should be installed with a sensitivity device to prevent them from going off inappropriately.

LOCKS:

If you've ever accidentally locked your keys in your car, you know how simple it is to slip a bent wire hanger through the rubber frame of your windows, hook it onto your door lock, and lift the lock up; simple, that is, if your door locks are those "golf-tee-like" protuberances that pop up from the top of your door. To discourage a car thief, replace those easy-to-open door push-button knobs with flangeless "hidden" locks.

You can take extra precautions by having additional lock systems installed on other parts of your car. To protect tires from being stolen, you can replace one lug nut on each tire with a locking nut that you release with a special key. Special locking devices are also available for some hubcaps—such as spoked wheel covers.

There are two schools of thought when it comes to adding locks to your car: (1) You should buy locks that a would-be thief can't locate and/or figure out, so that he'll get discouraged and change his mind about taking your car; or (2) You should buy locks that are out in the open so that even if a car thief knows how to break into the lock system, he won't want to bother to take the extra time to do it.

"Hidden" locks: Ignition locks can be installed in a reinforced steering column or in the dashboard for as little as $100. Hood locks prevent thieves from getting into the car's engine compartment, a great defense for two reasons: if they'd planned to bypass the ignition switch from that angle, they can't get underneath the hood to do so; and if you *have* an alarm or other antitheft device underneath the hood, they can't get in to shut it off. Hood locks range in price from about $35 for do-it-yourself installation to over $100 for more sophisticated models. Heavy-duty chain locks may be installed inside your trunk and operated by your key.

Visible locks: One of the more common visible locks is a "cane" lock—a steel rod, shaped like a "C," that hooks around your steering wheel and brake pedal. They are inexpensive (about $10) and though many thieves can easily cut them off, they may assume that you have other devices as well and, frightened of spending extra time, will move on. Guard plates installed over your trunk lock with carriage bolts will protect the trunk's lock cylinder. Switch locks are key-operated electrical switches, like an ignition switch, that turn your alarm system on and off. If placed on the outside of the car, with the face of the switch obvious but the connections on the back inaccessible, a thief may see that the car is alarmed and so this switch alone may be enough to deter him.

STEREO ANTITHEFT DEVICES:
   The higher the quality of your car's stereo system, the more likely that it will be stolen. Now, in order to discourage thieves, many luxury car manufacturers have begun to install stereo systems that "won't work" if they're removed from the dashboard of the car in which they were first installed. The systems vary from those controlled by a secret digital computer code, to a system that is controlled by the owner's door key.
   You can also buy some stereo components—including tape decks, radios, and speakers—that "snap-out," so you can take them with you after you've parked your car. Or, you can install alarms on the stereo equipment itself. Whatever your choice, remember that it's unwise to spend a lot of money on a terrific sound system without spending at least a little money to protect it.

Driving Habits That Safeguard Your Car

   Besides using antitheft devices, there are ways that you can help to prevent your car from being stolen that require nothing more than common sense and an alert mind.

☐   Never leave your car running and unattended either when warming up the car or when doing quick errands.

☐   When parking your car, always lock the doors, close the windows, and take your keys.

☐   If your keys have "punch-out" numbers, these should be removed and kept at home for reference in case you lose them. If the numbers are left on the keys, thieves, parking lot attendants, and others who have access to your car could use these numbers to duplicate your keys.

☐ Lock any packages or tempting equipment (CB radios, tape decks, stereo speakers, etc.) in the trunk, when possible, or take them with you when you leave the car.

☐ If you're parking on a street, always turn your wheels in toward the curb. This makes it much harder to tow the car, as some car thieves may try to do.

☐ Park under a streetlight, if possible.

☐ If you have a garage, park your car inside and lock the garage and the car. This good habit protects the car from harsh weather as well as from theft.

☐ If you park in a public parking garage, take your parking lot ticket with you. Leaving it in the car allows a thief to exit the parking lot without being challenged by a parking lot attendant. Never leave your license in the car because a thief could use this document to impersonate you to a police officer. Give the parking lot attendant *only* your ignition key, or else you may invite theft of your trunk.

☐ Remember to *activate* any antitheft device you have installed; they won't do you much good if they're not set to go.

☐ To help in recovering your car if it is stolen, put your Vehicle Identification Number (VIN), located on your registration, in different hidden spots on your car—under your hood, behind the fenders, inside your car doors, in the trunk. You can use a vibrating pencil or electric etcher to imprint the number permanently, or for a "better-than-nothing approach," use a crayon simply to write the number anywhere that seems convenient.

Auto theft, like most crimes, is one of those unpleasant areas about which most people prefer to think "It will never happen to me." If you're lucky, it won't; but, taking the simple precautions described above can help to ensure that your car will remain *your* car until the day you choose to sell it.

Personal Safety

At some point when you're driving, you may take a wrong turn and end up in an unfamiliar, dangerous area. Possibly in your own neighborhood you may feel your car is being followed, or your safety is threatened on a dark street where you can't see in front of your car very clearly. Even the brief moments you're stopped at a traffic light can be long enough for a skilled thief to reach through a window and steal your wallet, shopping bags, or other valuables off a passenger seat.

Planning ahead is the best way to thwart such attempts and to steer away from such situations unharmed. Here are some suggestions to keep in mind.

☐ Keep your windows rolled up, except for a small opening for ventilation if you're driving in a questionable, unfamiliar neighborhood. If you need to drive with the windows rolled down, at least keep all tempting objects out of sight—in the trunk or under a seat.

☐ While you're driving, if another driver tries to force you off the road by crowding you with his car, blow your horn to attract help. If you are forced over, try to back up and pull away, blowing your horn all the while. Try to keep your car in motion until you can drive off safely.

☐ If you suspect that someone is following you, turn down some busy streets; if the suspected auto proceeds behind you, drive to the nearest police or fire station or open store—never to your home.

☐ Try to park in a well-lighted area or under a streetlight.

☐ Always look in your car before you enter to make sure all is well.

☐ Lock your car whenever you leave it.

6
The Smart Driver's Guide to Buying a New (or Used) Car

If you're like most drivers, the day is going to come when you'll have to buy a car. Perhaps after years of being pampered, with the return to you of reliable performance, your car is finally giving in to the signs of old age—stalling, unexpected breakdowns, lack of pick-up. Or maybe, you're realizing that one car can no longer meet the demands of your growing family, and it's time to add a second car to your garage. In either case, you're going to have a long list of factors to consider before you buy—the first of which may be deciding whether you want a brand-new car or a used one. Both kinds of deals require preparation, including some research plus some strategic planning to ensure that the car in which you drive off is the one you *really* want and need. Let's consider the "game plan" for buying a new car.

To most people, a new car is *more* than just a car; it's a symbol of what they've achieved so far in their lives, and of what they expect of the future. Whether you drive a little red sports coupe, a roomy four-door sedan, or a family station wagon, your automobile can say a lot about your personality, as well as your lifestyle. It's also one of the largest purchases (in terms of cost) that you make in your lifetime, usually second only to a home.

No wonder, then, that most people are intimidated by the mere prospect of buying a new car. There you are, trying to choose among all the tantalizing new options to find a car that best suits your needs at a price that you can afford, while the dealer is trying to figure out how he can reap the biggest profit in selling you a car. The problem is, he has a lot more practice at this than you do. You buy a new car only a few times during your life; he *sells* new cars every day.

Ultimately, of course, the dealer wants you to be just as satisfied with your new purchase as you want to be; he just wants to put a higher price tag on that satisfaction than you want to pay. But, there are ways to outsmart a dealer, even those who are experts in the fine art of "hard sell," and that means doing some work ahead of time. The process of buying a car begins long before you even walk into a dealership. It begins the moment you first decide that you want a car, and continues through the first time that you pull it into your own driveway.

MAJOR QUESTIONS BEFORE SHOPPING AROUND

Before you even look at a single picture of a car, imagine what the perfect car for you would be like. Describe this car on paper, and in so doing, make sure you ask yourself the following questions.

☐ **WHAT CAN I AFFORD?** Check around at banks, and watch for manufacturers' newspaper advertisements for car financing, to get an idea of what monthly car loan payments will be like, what kind of interest rates you can expect to pay, and what kind of down payment is expected. Also, check out insurance rates for the cars you have in mind when figuring out your monthly costs. Balance these figures with your other monthly costs to get an idea of what price you could comfortably pay for a new car.

☐ **HOW WILL I USE THE CAR?** Do you spend most of the day driving, whether on business or for family errands? If so, size and comfort may be of major importance to you. If your car is just meant for commuting, to get you from home to the office or the train station, a small, fuel-efficient model may be more in order. Do you need lots of trunk space? Are you in a carpool? If so, you may opt for a more convenient four-door over a two-door model. If you use the car for work (as a salesperson or real estate agent, for example), you may be concerned about getting a car that will impress your clients, boost your own image. If this new car is going to be for long weekend getaways, you'll want one that's comfortable *and* fuel efficient.

☐ **WHAT KIND OF CLIMATE DO I LIVE IN?** If you live in the Rocky Mountains, for example, air conditioning probably isn't necessary, but four-wheel (or at least front-wheel) drive for improved traction in snow, disc brakes for dependability in wet weather, and a rear defogger probably are. On the other hand, if you live in a city with a year-round warm climate like Phoenix or Miami, air conditioning in your car might be a priority.

☐ **WHERE WILL I PARK THE CAR?** You may not want an expensive luxury car if you're going to park it on the streets of a major metropolitan area because it could be stolen. If you are going to use your car for quick runs to the grocery store or local shopping mall, keep in mind that crowded parking lots are prime spots for contracting nicks and scrapes on your car's body; that silver sports car might not be the most practical choice for you in this case.

☐ **WHAT SPECIAL CONCERNS DO I HAVE?** If you're six feet three inches tall, lots of leg room may be your most important concern; if you're five feet one inches, you may need power seats to help raise you to a comfortable driving level. Power windows and door locks may be especially important safety features if you tend to drive in not-so-safe neighborhoods. If you do lots of stop-and-go driving, and tend to parallel park frequently, power steering and brakes may be important features for you.

☐ **WHAT KINDS OF OPTIONS ARE IMPORTANT TO ME?** If your shortest drive is 500 miles, you may not be comfortable without cruise control. If you love music, you may want an excellent stereo/tape deck system. Maybe you live in Southern California and simply *must* have a sunroof.

Answer all these questions as completely as possible. Only by really thinking through all your options will you be most likely to buy the right car for your needs. Once you have an idea of the right car for you, the next step is to locate it in a dealer's showroom.

Narrowing Your Options

At this point, there's still no reason for you to begin bartering with a dealer; you're not adequately prepared yet. Now that you know what you want in a car, it's time to do some research to find what models meet your requirements.

☐ Talk to friends—particularly those who use their cars in the same way that you plan to use yours. Ask them what they like best—and least—about their cars and decide whether you're willing to live with the same things that they are. Ask what they would do differently if they were buying a car today.

☐ Read everything you can about the cars you're considering buying. The American Automobile Association (AAA) publishes evaluations for members called "Autograph" reports—available for free at most of their regional offices—in which they report on test drives they've taken of new models. Go to your local library and scan automobile magazines and consumer publications for news, critiques, test results, and any other information about any car you're considering. Write to car manufacturers to find out more about a car's special features. Read, discuss, compare, and evaluate all the cars that you're considering until you've narrowed down your options to three or four models.

□ Begin browsing in dealer showrooms. At this point, you want to begin taking test drives, which means you're going to begin to hear some of the dealer's high-pressure hype: "This is the last canary-yellow two-door convertible in all of the county and I've got two bids on it already. If you don't take it now, it's not going to be here tomorrow." You can just hold your ground and say "Well, that's fine; but until I test drive it —and a few other cars—I don't want to think about buying."

Now, however, it's time to decide if you really *do* want that canary-yellow convertible. What should you look for on the test drive? Shouldn't all new cars run like new? What differences are you supposed to be able to detect from one car to another? Contrary to popular opinion, a test drive is more than just a spin around the block. It's the time to determine if this automobile will meet your criteria for the best car for you.

HOW TO TAKE A TEST DRIVE

□ **HOW LONG SHOULD YOU TEST DRIVE A NEW CAR?** The length of time can vary; generally, a test drive should be at least an hour long, and some dealers will even allow you to take the car home overnight. A test drive should take as long as necessary for you to feel that you really have a good idea of how this particular car operates.

□ **WHERE SHOULD YOU GO?** Try to immerse the car in as many different situations as you might reasonably expect to drive in under normal circumstances. Drive it on the highway as well as on neighborhood streets. Take it to the grocery store and load up the trunk with grocery bags, if that's what you'd normally use the car for; take the kids along if you're likely to become the official "chauffeur" for junior high activities.

□ **WHAT SHOULD YOU LOOK FOR?** There are four general categories: performance, safety, comfort, and economy.

Performance: Do you feel comfortable, in control, when you're driving this car? Does the steering handle well? Do the gears shift easily? Are the brakes smooth and quick to respond? Do the accessories work well? (You should test them *all.*) Try out the windshield wipers and washer, lights and turn signals, and all the other essentials. Does the car have good pick-up after a stop—even if you're running the air conditioner? Is the car noisy when you reach high speeds? How well are bumps in the road buffeted?

Safety: Try to find out how the car rated in the government crash tests (information available from the National Highway Traffic Safety Administration). Take note if the dashboard is padded, if all the door knobs and window handles are nonprotruding, so they'll be less likely to cause injury in case of an accident. Do the seat belts work well? Is the car equipped with air bags? Make sure the headrests are adjustable. Look for special features such as anti-lacerative windshields and antilock brakes. Make sure the dashboard is well illuminated for night driving. Check to see that all mirrors are adjustable.

Comfort: Make sure there's enough room for you and any anticipated passengers in the car. Think ahead: will there still be enough room if, in two years, you have another baby?; or decide to buy that St. Bernard you've been wanting? Do you like the upholstery?; will it be easy to clean? Can you easily reach the accelerator, brake, and all switches on the dashboard? Are the seats easy to adjust?

Economy: On the window of the car, there should be a sticker that tells you the estimated miles per gallon of fuel that this car can expect to get during both highway driving and city driving, as rated by the EPA. These estimates will vary depending on how you drive, but you can still compare them from car to car to determine the most fuel-efficient vehicle. A good city rating is about 25 mpg (miles per gallon); on the highway, look for a car with a rating of at least 35 mpg.

Remember that many options—power door locks, windows, brakes, and steering; air conditioning, defrosters—can cut down on fuel efficiency by adding extra weight to the car, so you should carefully balance the benefits of each before you buy. If you want air conditioning, ask whether it has an automatic shut-off switch so that your air conditioner will not operate when the accelerator pedal is fully depressed. This feature allows full engine power for maximum passing safety on highways.

Test drive as many different cars as you feel necessary until you have decided on one particular car. Remember that you don't have to limit yourself to just one test drive per car. Sometimes, after test driving one car, you'll notice things you forgot to look for on a past test drive and you'll want to go back and retest drive a car. Feel entitled to do this. You can never be *too* sure about this important purchase.

WAYS TO OUTTALK A CAR DEALER

At last, you've filtered through all the information available on all the wonderful new cars in which you're interested and have focused on that one car for you. Now you have to face the challenging part: getting that special car at a price you can afford. Keep in mind that car dealers *expect* you to bargain for a better price on a car, and you're cheating yourself if you don't. But before you even enter into a discussion with a car dealer, there are some negotiation strategies you should be aware of:

☐ **FIND OUT THE DEALER COST OF THE CAR.** Once you've decided on the particular car you want to buy, ask a librarian to show you the new car price guides available. Most will list not only the manufacturer's suggested list price of the car, but also the price that the dealer paid for the car. It is this dealer cost—sometimes 20 percent less than the suggested retail price—that is your bottom line for negotiation. Sometimes you can also get this information by asking the dealer to see his factory invoice for the car. The dealer doesn't have to show you this invoice, but many dealers will be agreeable. Remember, the dealer will always make some profit. Even if he sells you the car at his cost, he's entitled to a rebate known as a "dealer kickback" from the manufacturer. So, if the car lists for $10,000, but the dealer paid $8,000 for it, you should begin bargaining up from $8,000, not down from $10,000.

☐ **NEVER LET THE DEALER KNOW HOW MUCH YOU CAN SPEND.**
It's the first question he'll ask you, and it's the *one* question you
should never answer, although you should always be aware of
what you can comfortably afford. The fact that you're interested in only certain models of cars should be a big enough
clue for the dealer as to how much you can afford.

☐ **WATCH OUT FOR THE SECOND STICKER.** This dealer practice
reached a peak several years ago when imports of Japanese cars
were restricted, and now is not as common among car dealers.
But, particularly in some metropolitan areas, you may still
have to be careful. For certain cars in great demand, dealers
may mark up the manufacturer's retail price and display this
second price in a sticker on the window, beside the usual manufacturer's sticker. In the past, some markups were as high as
$15,000 and were usually identified with some cryptic remark:
ADP ("additional dealer profit"), ADM ("additional dealer
markup"), "pre-delivery inspection," or "dealer preparation."
These latter two terms infer that the dealer has done additional
inspections of the car before selling it, and he is accounting for
the costs of these inspections. In fact, if these inspections are
performed at all, their cost is already included in the basic
price of most cars. The fine print on the manufacturer's price
sticker acknowledges this.

It is legal for dealers to add these costs, though they have to
make it clear to you what they're doing; this second sticker is
enough to make it clear, according to the law, but it's up to
you to be aware of what it means. Avoid dealers who resort to
second stickers; you'd be better off driving out-of-town to a
rural dealership than to buy from a dealer who uses second
stickers.

☐ **LEARN TO NEGOTIATE ON THE OPTIONS.** After you've made
your initial bid on a car (basing it, as mentioned before, on the
dealer's cost of the car), the dealer will undoubtedly try to get
you to go much higher on the price. You need to have specific
details to be able to negotiate down a price, and these details
are to be found in the car's options.

First, make sure that any options on the car are manufacturer-installed rather than dealer-installed. Dealer-installed options are generally more expensive and of lower quality than those installed by the manufacturer or an outside party. If certain options (such as stereos, sunroofs, etc.) are dealer-installed, they'll be on a sticker beside the manufacturer's sticker, listing all the options that are standard on the car. Tell the dealer you want the same car but without these options. Chances are, he won't have such a car in the shop and will tell you so. At this point, tell him that you'll have to look elsewhere for a car that doesn't have these added costly options. Often, at this point, a dealer will offer to lower the costs of some of these options in order to get you to buy the car from him, rather than from another dealer, so you'll be on your way to a price you can afford.

Also, beware of options that you don't need. If the dealer sticker notes that $150 covers the cost of fabric sealant, for example, remember that you can get the same results by buying an aerosol can of fabric sealant in the hardware store and spraying it over the car interior yourself. Point this fact out to your dealer. Tell him you refuse to pay for this service and he should be willing to delete this cost; hence, the price of the car will be reduced another $150.

If the car has an elaborate, dealer-installed stereo system, tell the dealer you'd prefer to buy a car with no stereo system, and buy one yourself later at an automotive stereo shop. (It's a good idea, anyway; most automotive supplies stores or stereo shops have less expensive, higher-quality stereos than you would be able to get from a dealer.) The dealer may not be willing to remove the stereo from the car, but he may be willing to slash part of the cost of the stereo off the total cost of the car.

□ **GET THE FINAL OFFERING PRICE IN WRITING.** Once you've gotten a dealer down to a price that you feel is fair, ask him to put his offer of a price in a signed letter of agreement; then tell him you want to "sleep on it." Leave the showroom and prepare to do some comparative shopping.

☐ **CALL UP ALL THE DEALERS IN YOUR AREA** who sell the car you're interested in buying and tell them the price quote you've already gotten. Ask them if they will offer you a lower price. If they do, plan to buy the car from them; if no other dealer will offer you a price as low as the original dealer, then you know you've made a good deal.

☐ **COMPARE WARRANTIES AND SERVICE CONTRACTS.** All new cars come with a warranty. The most common warranty on a new car is for one year or the first 12,000 miles—meaning that the manufacturer will cover the costs of any repairs made within this time. High-priced luxury cars generally have longer warranties than more modestly priced ordinary cars.

Usually dealers will try to sell you "extended warranties" or service contracts in addition to the warranty that comes with the car. These contracts will extend the provisions of the original contract for a longer amount of time, but this security comes with a very steep price tag. Service contracts can run as high as several hundred dollars. When you're comparing the price of the service contract (say $500) with the overall price of the car (say $13,000) it will seem small in comparison, which is why, generally speaking, you should *never* buy a service contract at the same time you buy your car. In most cases, the service contracts end up costing more than the repairs that they cover. Wait until your original warranty nears its expiration date, when you have a better idea of how well the car runs and how much it costs to repair, before considering buying an extended warranty or service contract.

☐ **FINANCING THE CAR.** Most dealers will also try to get you to finance the car through their manufacturer's financing program; sometimes these programs are worthwhile. But be sure to compare the manufacturer's financing with that of local banks. The difference in interest rates can vary greatly.

Probably the most important thing you have to do in order to get the best deal on a new car is to rearrange the way you *think* about buying a car. Don't think of yourself as being at the mercy of a car dealer, as all too many consumers do. Remember that you're the one who is in control; you know what you want and how much you can afford. Your greatest weapon is your ability to turn around and walk out of the showroom at any time. Make sure that the dealer knows you're willing to do this, and you'll remain in control of the situation; and chances are, you'll get that special car you want at a better price than you thought possible.

BREAKING IN A NEW CAR

Few feelings are as satisfying as the first time you slide into the driver's seat of a new car, turn on the ignition, pull out of the dealership, and think to yourself, "This is all mine." There's something magical about the experience. You look down at the odometer and see mostly zeros. Through the windshield, you note how the sun glimmers on your spotless new hood, and inside the seats seem uncommonly soft and pliable. On the dashboard are symbols that you have yet to learn about completely, yet you know, in a few weeks' time, they'll be as familiar to you as the face of your wristwatch. Then there's the smell of brand-new vinyl or fabric upholstery, which reminds you each time you enter the car of the priceless treasure you possess.

A new automobile seems to have boundless potential, and you'll want to drive it all over town to show it off, to enjoy the excitement and pleasure of driving a new car. Under these circumstances it's easy to forget that a new car, like a new pair of new shoes, needs to be broken in gently. Actually it will take months—and a few thousand miles—before all the parts of your automobile wear comfortably into each other; excessive early wear can make a part fail before its time. No matter what you do, your car will probably run well for its first 40,000 miles or so; but if you abuse your car when it's new, you may be creating problems for yourself when your car hits 60,000 miles and upward. Operating with care and caution can mean fewer repairs and better, longer-lasting performance when your car is no longer the sparkling new machine it once was.

Most cars are considered well broken-in at 4,000 miles; but

the most crucial part of the break-in period is the first 1,000 miles, because that's when the parts do most of their "wearing-in" to one another.

For example, during the first few times you drive your car, new brakes need to be properly burnished (gradually contoured). New linings or disc-brake pads don't exactly match the contours of the brake drums. If only a little piece of the lining or pad touches the metal when new, a sudden stop or "jolt" could cause that small contact area to overheat and leave a hard, slick surface on that particular spot of the brake lining or pad. Forever after, that part of the braking system will be more slippery than other parts and braking will be uneven. However, if in the first few thousand miles of driving, all braking is done gently and evenly, the uneven parts of new brake linings or pads will gradually level off so its full surface will contact the metal and braking should be even and smooth thereafter.

Similar scenarios can be drawn for the tires, transmission gears, clutch linings—even the air-conditioning and heating systems. It's important to "exercise" your car, take it through its complete repertoire of operations—stops, accelerations, moderate-length drives at moderate speeds—to ensure that all car parts wear together uniformly. Check your owner's manual to see if it offers specific recommendations for breaking in your particular car. Many do not, but still have vital information to help you understand how your new automobile runs. Following is a step-by-step guide that could help you to break in your new car safely and to ensure long-lasting, reliable performance from all your car systems.

☐ **WATCH YOUR SPEEDS AND DISTANCES.** For the first 500 miles, drive under 50 mph; if possible, drive a minimum of 50 miles at a time so the car gets completely warmed up.

On cold mornings, allow the engine to warm up for two minutes to allow the oil to get circulating throughout the engine. If possible, in cold weather, keep your new car in a warm garage; the engine and charging system have to work harder in cold weather and starting up too fast on several cold mornings consecutively could cause excessive wear on parts. One positive note: generally it's better to break in a car in winter than summer because there's less chance of its overheating.

Avoid short distance, quick trips (to a nearby store, for example) and never let the engine idle excessively once it's warmed up. If you plan to use your car for commuting from home to office, you may want to get up early and drive the car for an extra fifteen minutes or so, taking detours away from stop-and-go traffic so you can safely monitor your car's accelerations and decelerations. When going uphill, keep the engine working easily by downshifting to a lower gear. Try to take similar detours on your way home. If you live in a city, take a few "break-in trips" of no less than 50 miles, driving on country roads if possible, where traffic is minimal and you can keep your speed to below 50 mph. If your car has a tachometer (see glossary), try to keep the rpms low—no more than half of the maximum engine speed marked in red on the gauge's face.

From 500–1000 miles, gradually increase the maximum speed, slightly, up to 55 mph, to about three quarters of the maximum recommended rpms, and begin some highway driving. You can shorten your minimum length trip to 25 miles and eliminate the two-minute warm-up. After 1,000 miles, you can occasionally accelerate the car full throttle and drive, virtually, as far as you want.

☐ **NEVER TOW A TRAILER** during the first 1,000 miles you drive your car, and try to avoid excessive weight in the form of passengers or cargo since both these factors can cause unnecessary strain on your engine's parts.

☐ **CHANGE ALL FLUIDS AND THEIR FILTERS**—including transmission, coolant, and oil—when you've driven 1,000 miles and again at 4,000 miles, and continue to change the oil every 3,000 miles thereafter. This step is vitally important to the break-in process because oil (and less importantly your auto's other fluids) flows throughout your engine, ensuring that no two parts wear against one another and create too much heat. But as your auto parts are leveling off against one another, tiny fragments of metal are being shaved off and can be circulated throughout the engine in your oil. Eventually, these microscopic metal pieces can cause engine parts to wear too quickly. Obviously, it's also important to change your oil filter when you change your oil so that you're not pumping clean oil through a dirty filter, and so that your filter doesn't become overloaded and allow the metal filings to circulate back out into your oil.

Also, when your car is new, be especially careful to check your oil level regularly. New cars use more oil than broken-in cars because the joining of oil-retaining surfaces inside the engine is not yet complete. As a result, oil is consumed in the combustion process at a higher rate than it will be later. Don't wait until you see your dashboard "Oil" light go on before you add oil; by the time it goes on—or by the time you *notice* it —engine parts could have rubbed against one another dry, and some damage could have already been done. Instead, just make it a regular habit to check your oil level yourself. (See page 21 for "How to check your oil.") Never let your oil fall more than a quart short.

☐ **AVOID HARD, ABRUPT BRAKING.** Initial "roughness" in brakes is normal, but by 500 miles, your brakes should feel smooth when you press the brake pedal. Squeaks, grinding noises, or "jerkiness" when you depress the pedal could signal deeper mechanical difficulties, and you should consult a mechanic or your dealer.

Don't be afraid to slam on the brakes in an unavoidable emergency, of course. It makes poor sense to "baby" the brakes if it will mean a crash resulting in harm to passengers as well as your car.

☐ **CHECK TIRE INFLATION.** Don't assume that just because your car is new, that your tires are properly inflated. Often they aren't, and improperly inflated tires will wear out faster than properly inflated tires—especially if they're underinflated. If the car rides too roughly, and seems not to take bumps easily in the road, your tires are probably overinflated. If you seem to have trouble going around curves, your tires are probably underinflated—they'll probably look more squat or bulgy at the bottom, too (unless they're radial tires, which usually bulge a bit more than other tires anyway). Underinflated tires will wear badly on the edges of the tread; overinflated tires will wear badly in the center. Remember always to check tire pressure when tires are cold. (See page 10 for "How to check tire pressure.")

Also, keep aware of how well balanced your wheels are. If your seat seems to vibrate, you may have rear-tire imbalance; if your steering wheel vibrates you may have front-tire imbalance. In either case, you should have the wheels checked out by your mechanic or dealer. (For more information about wheel balance and alignment, see page 15.)

☐ **USE YOUR ACCESSORIES WITH CAUTION.** Air conditioning, cruise control, heater, tape deck, and radio—all these systems need to be broken in slowly, and they should be used frequently to do so. However, just as you shouldn't run your car for too long a period of time, don't overuse your accessories right away, or switch them on and off too frequently in their first few weeks of use. The individual parts of their systems have to wear in gradually. When using any of these accessories, keep a close eye on temperature gauges to watch for overheating, particularly if you're breaking in your new car in summertime or hot temperatures.

☐ **PROTECT THE BODY OF YOUR CAR** by not washing it too soon. It takes thirty days for body paint to get totally hard and become impervious to most of the hazards of the road. So, during the first month, avoid any harsh detergents. Always avoid car washes with sharp brushes; look for car washes that have sponge- or rag-type cleaners that are changed regularly, since dirt embedded in sponges or cloths can scratch a car's finish just as easily as hard brushes.

To protect your car's interior, buy car mats right away to preserve your car's carpeting, and install little plastic garbage bags on your door handles. If you have vinyl seats, be sure not to park your car in direct sunlight, since vinyl can gradually deteriorate when exposed frequently to heat and ultraviolet rays. If you have fabric upholstery, a fabric-guard spray can make the seats more resistant to spills and stains.

Learning to drive and care for your car with the respect it deserves right from the first day you own it will not only improve your car's performance, it may help you to maintain that pride and satisfaction you felt the first day you drove your car home.

WHERE TO GET HELP IF YOUR CAR IS A "LEMON"

New cars can give you a great sense of comfort and security; they're supposed to "run like new" and therefore provide worry-free traveling for at least the first year or so of use. Almost always, a new car *does* operate as well as it should, and mechanical problems don't start until *long* after the warranty runs out.

But every now and then, a "lemon," with all kinds of built-in problems, rolls off the assembly line onto a dealer's floor, and ultimately, into the driveway of some innocent, unsuspecting buyer. You may realize it the first time you go out on the highway for a leisurely drive when suddenly, with a few mighty backfires, the car just "dies." At first you may think, "No problem. My warranty is still fresh; I'll just take the car back to the dealer who'll have it fixed in no time."

Three months later, after numerous trips to the dealership, followed by still more highway stall-outs, you will undoubtedly be less forgiving or hopeful and have to face the hard cold truth: your shiny new car is, in fact, a "lemon."

Today, new car owners have several options if they have the misfortune of buying a "lemon" (so-called because such repeat breakdowns can leave a "sour taste in one's mouth"). Almost all major manufacturers (Mercedes-Benz is the exception) participate in some sort of arbitration program to solve owner/dealer/manufacturer disputes. "Lemon laws," the first of which was passed in Connecticut in 1982, have now been established in thirty-nine states and the District of Columbia, and they're under consideration in other state legislatures.

"Lemon laws" are designed to help consumers and manufacturers resolve disputes quickly, and with a minimum amount of cost to both parties. The laws vary slightly from state to state but generally, they define a "lemon" as: an automobile that has a defect that substantially impairs its use, for which a repair has been unsuccessfully attempted at least four times, or that has caused the car to be out-of-service (in a repair garage) for thirty days or more during the first 12,000 miles, or first year of use (whichever comes first).

The laws also require the car owner to file a complaint with the manufacturer during the warranty period (although the case can be argued and resolved *after* the warranty expires). Most laws also require that the case be settled within forty days after the complaint is made and some laws offer the car owner an additional option for a twenty-day mediation period in which a compromise might be reached without actually entering into full arbitration.

The first step to take if you're convinced your car is a "lemon" is to file a formal complaint with the manufacturer. You can do this in one of two ways:

(1) Write the manufacturer's customer complaint bureau directly (the address will probably be in your owner's manual).

(2) Ask your dealer for the name and number of the manufacturer's "zone representative" for your area.

Simultaneously, you should also send a copy of your complaint to your local Better Business Bureau office and/or to your state attorney general's office. If arbitration ends up being unsuccessful, you may be able to seek help from these sources.

Generally, there are three different types of arbitration programs that manufacturers work with: AUTOCAP ("*Auto*mobile *C*onsumer *A*ction *P*rogram); Autoline, (an automotive arbitration program within the Council of Better Business Bureaus); or, as in the case of Ford and Chrysler, arbitration boards that the manufacturers themselves set up. The program that your manufacturer uses will usually be outlined in the car's warranty manual, and sometimes right on the warranty sticker on the car.

According to guidelines set up by the Federal Trade Commission (FTC), members of these arbitration panels must be objective and have no personal interest in the case; and two thirds of the panel must be from outside the automotive industry. (AUTOCAP, which is sponsored by the National Automobile Dealers Association, does not abide by the FTC guidelines and requires only *half* its members to be from outside the industry, although no panel member can be affiliated with the manufacturer in question in a particular case.) Also, according to the FTC, the car owner cannot be charged a fee for filing for arbitration (though it's recommended that you consult a lawyer); and the arbitration panel's resolution must be quick and fair. Most panel members are trained volunteers from the community, many of whom have some experience dealing with consumer rights.

After you've filed your complaint, you'll be offered a chance to try a twenty-day mediation program. During this time, a representative from the arbitration program will collect all the facts from you, your dealer, and the manufacturer, and try to develop a compromise that will satisfy all three parties. Most recent consumer complaints have been resolved through this mediation without ever having to be brought before the board.

If you are unhappy with the compromise suggested by the arbitration panel's representative during mediation, you *can* reject it, and opt to enter into arbitration. Depending on the particular program, you or your lawyer may be able to present your case in person at an arbitration hearing, or you may only be able to submit all your evidence in writing and the panel will review it privately and suggest a resolution. Resolutions may vary from full replacement of the car, to refund of the price of the car, less the usage already derived from it, to a simple requirement of trying to fix the problem one more time.

Happily, the track records of all three types of arbitration programs seem to point in favor of the consumer; most car owners report being satisfied with the outcome of their arbitration process. If, however, you are not satisfied with the arbitration panel's recommendation, you have the right to appeal the case and to sue the manufacturer in public court.

If you're like most car owners, you'll never have to enter into arbitration at all. Your new car will meet your expectations for performance. But it doesn't hurt to think ahead, and to be ready if something does go wrong. Here are some suggestions to follow that can help make any arbitration go smoothly, and work best for you:

☐ Keep records of every transaction you have with your dealer and/or repair facility, whether or not you think it's applicable to the particular problem in question; furthermore, arrange these documents in chronological order.

☐ Keep all original copies of your repair records and send only photocopies of these records to the manufacturer, dealer, arbitration board, etc.

☐ Familiarize yourself with the "lemon law" in your state, as well as the requirements of your manufacturer's arbitration program. Remember that even if your state does not have a "lemon law," you can still enter into arbitration.

☐ Before the arbitration hearing or panel meeting, ask the arbitration representative for copies of all documents submitted by the dealer and/or manufacturer, allowing enough time to respond to these reports if you want.

If you need additional advice, there is a consumer group set up specifically to help car owners deal with automotive arbitration proceedings:

AID FOR LEMON OWNERS
21711 West Ten Mile Road
Suite 210
Southfield, Michigan 48075

In addition, you can get a list of lawyers in your area who specialize in auto repair problems by sending a self-addressed, stamped envelope to:

THE CENTER FOR AUTO SAFETY
2001 S Street NW
Suite 410
Washington, D.C. 20009

In the future, if some consumer advocates get their way, there might be a federal "lemon law" that would either amend or replace the state laws currently in effect. There's no doubt that successful arbitration takes some conscientious effort on your part, but most car owners who have experienced it will tell you the time and effort are well spent. You're responsible, to a great extent, for your own satisfaction; if you're unhappy with a new car (or, for that matter, *any* new purchase), it's up to you to report your dissatisfaction to the proper authorities. To use an old saying that's a favorite among auto buffs: "The squeaky wheel gets the grease."

BUYING A USED CAR

As prices for new cars soar ever higher, more and more drivers are looking into buying used cars that can give them the performance and reliability they need at a price they can afford. Not only is the initial cost of buying the car lower than a new car price, but insurance rates for used cars are also generally much more affordable than those for new cars.

However, those benefits come with risks, and buying a used car can require even more caution than buying a new car. There's always that dreadful chance that you could spend lots of money and end up with someone else's headache. You can lessen your risks for such disaster by reading up on the models in which you're interested, by examining any potential buys carefully, and by letting your mechanic go over the car even more thoroughly.

Finding Out What You Want and Can Afford

One unique advantage to buying a used car over a brand-new model is that the used car has a "track" record. Since time alone can tell whether a car is going to go down in history as a "clunker" or a "classic," a used car buyer has time on his or her side. Many consumer-oriented magazines publish car "issues" in which they list their "good bets" and "cars to avoid" in the used car sections. Also, simply asking acquaintances who drive cars similar to the one you're considering buying, about what they like—and dislike—about their autos can give clues for problems to look for in any potential buy.

Once you have a general idea of the kind of car you want to buy, investigate the classified ads of recent issues of your local paper and consult the "Blue Book" published by the National Automobile Dealers Association (NADA) in your bank or public library to find out the going rates for the cars in which you're interested. Keep in mind that you can usually bargain a seller down by 10 to 15 percent of his asking price.

Where to Shop

Once you have an idea of cars you like and can afford, there are four places you can look for them: used car dealers, new car dealers selling "trade-ins," rental companies, and private sellers.

☐ **USED CAR DEALERS AND NEW CAR DEALERS** offer the greatest selection of cars, but they also are most skilled in striking the best deal—for themselves. To ensure that a dealer is reputable, check to see if he is a member of either the NADA or the National Independent Automobile Dealers Association. Also, make sure that any car you're considering buying from a dealer has a "Buyers Guide" in the window. This is a legal document, required of the dealer by federal law, that will become part of your sales contract if you decide to buy the car. It will tell you if the car carries a warranty, what after-sale repairs the dealer will pay for and which ones you'd be responsible for, and if the car is being sold "as is" (in which case there is no warranty and there is a good chance something is wrong with the car; usually it's best to avoid "as is" cars).

☐ **BUYING FROM A RENTAL COMPANY** is usually a safe—though often expensive—way to buy a used car. The cars are usually only about a year old, but they've been driven long distances, as much as 25,000 miles, by many different rental customers. Almost all of them have good warranties (some companies will cover the cost of major repairs for up to two years after the car has been sold) and often you can request a maintenance history of the car so that you can see before you buy exactly what repairs have already been made on the car. Rental cars tend to cost slightly more than the "book value" of the used car because often they are "loaded" with accessories, and usually the price is not negotiable; the selection of used rental cars is not as great as at car dealers.

□ **BUYING FROM A PRIVATE INDIVIDUAL** can be the riskiest way to buy, but also offers the best chance of getting a great bargain. The best car deals are usually those you buy from people you know and trust, when you're familiar with the car's history and have a good idea of how well it runs. But even buying from a total stranger can be a rewarding experience if you act carefully.

First rule: no matter where you buy your used car, have your own mechanic look it over *before* you buy. Most mechanics will charge between $30 and $50 for this service—a fee that could save you a lot of money in the long run if the car turns out to be a "lemon." Beware of any dealer or private seller who doesn't allow you to take the car to your own mechanic for pre-purchase inspection.

How to Spot a Lemon

In addition to your mechanic's examination, there are many problems that you may be able to spot yourself. Here's a checklist of some points to remember.

BEFORE YOU GET IN THE CAR:
□ Look at the car in daylight; night and fog can impair visibility and hide imperfections. Bring along someone (your spouse, friend, even a mechanic) to help you. There's safety in numbers, and two people are more likely to spot trouble than one.

□ Examine the car's body for peeling, blistered, or uneven paint. Peeling and blistered paint may indicate a rust problem. Also check for rust in the trunk area and under the hood.

Uneven paint could mean major body work has been done on the car, indicating that it was in an accident, which could mean trouble for the car's performance.

☐ Test shock absorbers by pushing down on each corner of the car; if the shocks are in good shape, the car should bounce only once.

☐ Lift the hood. Check the belts, hoses, and battery for cracks and leaks. Make sure that the engine looks "clean." Excess oil on engine parts could also signal cracks and leaks in parts.

☐ Examine the tires—including the spare—for excessive and uneven wear; uneven wear could mean mechanical problems in the car.

☐ Bend under the car to look at the muffler, exhaust pipe, and tailpipe for corrosion; shake the tailpipe lightly to make sure it's secure.

☐ Carefully check the windows, windshields, mirrors, and lights for cracks. Test to make sure all lights and directional signals work.

☐ Look at the driveway under the car for drips. Brown fluid could mean an oil leak; green fluid could mean a radiator leak; clear fluid is probably just water from air-conditioner condensation and is no problem.

INSIDE THE CAR:
☐ Look for wear and tear on upholstery and floorboards, and broken springs in the seats.

☐ Turn on the ignition. Make sure all the dashboard lights and signals work well. Does the engine start up without hesitation? Check the windows, seat belts, windshield wipers, radio, and air conditioning to make sure they work.

☐ Pump on the accelerator pedal a little and watch the smoke come out of the exhaust pipe through your rearview mirror (or have your companion look for you). White smoke usually means a well-running engine; black smoke may just indicate that the carburetor needs adjusting—no serious problem; blue smoke may mean serious engine trouble—a car to avoid.

☐ Take a test drive according to the guidelines outlined earlier in this chapter, pages 153–55. *Never* buy a car if the seller won't let you test drive it.

☐ Don't expect the car to be perfect; few used cars are problem-free, but some problems are worse than others. When your mechanic checks the car, if he finds only minor problems, ask him to estimate the repair costs; if he sees major problems, keep looking for another car.

Driving a Hard Bargain

A smart car seller will always ask for a higher price than he thinks the car is worth. It's your job to figure out how to get him down into a reasonable price range. Consider these bargaining strategies:

☐ Act disinterested. The less interested you appear in the car, the more likely the seller will want to lower the price to entice you more.

☐ Focus on options that you don't need. ("Those racing stripes on the body may have cost you a lot of money, but I'd prefer the car without them.")

☐ Worry aloud about potential problems. ("It'll cost at least one hundred dollars to replace that broken blinker—and I'll need to cover up that spot where the upholstery is torn.")

☐ Use your mechanic's estimated minor repair costs in bargaining. ("I'll need a new alternator and it will run one hundred dollars; you'll have to lower your price by that much or I won't buy.")

☐ Beware of a car that is really *under*priced. It probably has some serious problem that you can't see.

☐ Get everything in writing. Make sure you receive a mileage disclosure statement before the seller transfers the car's title to you. This is your protection in case the odometer has been tampered with—a major concern when buying a used car. Also, if the dealer or private seller makes any promises to repair the car that are not already in the Buyers Guide or sales contract, ask him to add them to the sales contract *before* you sign. Oral agreements are very hard to enforce legally.

7
Auto Insurance:
Choices You Can Make

Some people assume that their auto insurance plan should last the life of their car. When they buy their new car, they choose the best deal from a handful of insurers and send out their biannual premium checks year after year, never questioning whether a better plan might have surfaced in the meantime.

It may be better to think of your auto insurance as you might your wardrobe: up for regular review and subject to change with your lifestyle. Many variables can influence the coverage, and costs, of the insurance you'll need—your age, where you live, the age and changing condition of your car, your driving habits, even your health. So it's worth your time and effort to call up different insurers every year or so to compare your current plan to other plans being offered and to consider how your personal insurance needs might have changed in the intervening years.

Begin by reviewing each kind of coverage available. There are eight basic kinds of insurance offered in most auto insurance "packages": bodily injury liability, property damage liability, medical payments, wage loss, substitute service, uninsured motorist, collision, and comprehensive.

LIABILITY INSURANCE

Most states require a car owner to carry liability insurance that will cover the costs of damages done to other people (bodily injury liability) or to their cars and/or property (property damage liability), up to a certain dollar amount covered in your policy. Most insurers will recommend that you buy more liability insurance than your state requires (which averages between $25,000 and $50,000), because for only a few extra dollars per payment, you can raise your liability insurance by as much as ten times the minimum required amount—a coverage that could save you thousands of dollars if you become involved in a serious accident. If a jury finds you guilty of causing a serious or fatal injury, your costs could run into the hundreds of thousands of dollars and if you're not adequately insured, you could be forced to sell some of your personal property to pay up. Even if you live in a state that requires "no-fault" insurance (see page 181) you will still need liability insurance to cover any possible big claims brought against you.

BODILY INJURY LIABILITY:

If you are involved in an accident in which someone is injured or killed, you could be held liable for that person's hospital and medical bills (including rehabilitation and nursing care), some monetary compensation for the victim's "pain and anguish," the salary that the victim is losing because of his inability to work due to the accident, and, in the case of death, funeral expenses. It's easy to see how these expenses can add up to a substantial amount of money.

PROPERTY DAMAGE LIABILITY:

This insurance covers the costs of damages you might do either to public or private property. Such an accident might involve another automobile, or it may mean that you've run into a highway sign or telephone pole—in which case you'd be responsible for the cost of replacing the property. This type of insurance would cover such costs.

Different insurance companies use different means to express their liability offerings. The two most common expressions are split-liability limits and single-liability limits.

Split liability is usually expressed as a group of three numbers. A typical example might be: 10/20/5 with the first two numbers referring to bodily injury liability insurance, and the last number referring to property damage. In this case, the "10" means that you would be covered for a maximum of $10,000 on injuries that you might cause to an individual, up to a maximum of $20,000 per accident (corresponding to the second numeral "20"). In other words, if you are in an accident with another car in which there was a driver and several passengers, your auto insurance would cover only $10,000 worth of injuries caused to any one passenger, and up to $20,000 for all injuries caused to all passengers. The "5" means that your company will pay out up to $5,000 to cover damage to someone else's property in an accident that was your fault.

Single liability is the option of having one lump sum to cover all your liability claims. The average minimum amount is $50,000, meaning that the company will pay up to $50,000 for all bodily injury and property damage liability costs.

MEDICAL PAYMENTS INSURANCE

Liability insurance covers the costs of medical treatments for injuries incurred by the driver and/or passengers of the *other* car. Medical payments insurance covers the costs of your own medical bills and those of the passengers in *your* car at the time of the accident. This coverage means that even if the accident was the other driver's fault, you don't have to sue him to collect; your insurance company will pay your medical costs, and if it's appropriate, they will try to collect payment from the other driver's insurance company.

The average minimum coverage of medical payments insurance is $500 per person in your car per accident, but most insurance experts suggest that you estimate possible medical costs to be $10,000 per person per accident and that you figure out your coverage by checking into how much your outside medical-hospital insurance plan would cover in case of an accident. Subtract that from $10,000 and the difference should be about what you'd want to get in medical payments insurance.

Keep in mind that usually your medical health insurance will cover only family members who might be passengers; if you carpool to work, or are often the neighborhood chauffeur for all the kids' activities, you may want to get more coverage than someone whose car is used primarily to transport only family members. If you live in a no-fault insurance state, you will be required to buy medical payments insurance (see page 181).

WAGE LOSS INSURANCE

This coverage is required of drivers who live in no-fault insurance states and is designed to compensate for salary you might lose because an injury has rendered you incapable of going to work, for a specified amount of time. Compensation is limited in the amount of money you can collect and the length of time you can collect it. Typically, an insurance company might pay you 85 percent of your salary up to a maximum of $200 per week for up to twenty-five weeks, making the maximum total payment $5,000. Again, you should carefully compare your wage loss insurance with the disability insurance allowed under your company's health insurance plan.

SUBSTITUTE SERVICE INSURANCE

Some—not all—no-fault states require that you buy substitute service coverage as well as wage loss insurance to cover the costs of tasks that you would normally do yourself but that now you have to pay someone else to do, such as housecleaning, child care, or gardening. Like wage loss insurance, the typical limit for substitute service benefits is $5,000.

UNINSURED MOTORIST INSURANCE

This insurance is an option of some companies in some states, and for certain situations, it could be a financial lifesaver. Liability laws require that if you're the victim of an accident caused by someone else, that other driver's liability insurance must pay the costs of your physical and property damage. But suppose that other driver is uninsured? Or underinsured? Or suppose you're the victim of a hit-and-run accident? Who pays then? Uninsured motorist coverage will usually pay for your medical expenses in these situations and, in some states, will also pay for damage to your property, including your car. This coverage is relatively inexpensive and since some sources estimate that 10 percent of all drivers in the United States are either uninsured or underinsured, the nominal costs of this coverage may be worth the extra peace of mind it will give you.

COLLISION INSURANCE

Collision coverage accounts for a big chunk of most insurance packages and is one of the areas where you can save the most money if you examine all your options and needs thoroughly. Collision insurance will cover the costs of repairs to your car—whether it was damaged in an accident with another automobile or by hitting some inanimate object such as a telephone pole. If your car is new or a high-priced model, it's important to be well covered with collision insurance since auto damages can greatly decrease the value of your car and be expensive to repair. If another driver rammed into your car, causing the damage, your insurance company might pay you and then sue the other driver's insurance company for reimbursement. In other cases, you may have to deal directly with the other driver's insurance company.

Insurance companies will pay collision compensation only up to the total retail value of your car and, like most medical insurance payments, you are expected to pay a deductible limit (ranging usually from $50 to $500) that you will have chosen when you initially buy your plan. Generally, it's best to take the highest deductible you can (up to, say, $500) because by doing so, you will lower your annual premiums.

Many people suggest that if your car is more than five years old, you drop collision insurance altogether, because the high cost of the insurance and the premiums may be more expensive than what you'd get back in insurance payments. The reason is simple: your insurance company will pay you for repairs only up to what the appraised value of your car is at the time of the accident. A five-year-old car, even in mint condition, is not worth as much as a brand-new car, yet it will cost the same to repair; but you won't get as much insurance money because the "book value" of your car has decreased by about one third of its new car value. The high premiums you'll be paying will be on the costs of your car when it was new, though when it comes time to collect collision insurance, you'll get only up to the book value of your car at the time of the accident.

COMPREHENSIVE INSURANCE

Comprehensive insurance is usually an optional coverage that will pay for damages to your car other than crash damages. Such incidents may include: if your car is stolen, vandalized, caught in a flood or fire, damaged from a falling object, or in a collision with an animal.

Costs of comprehensive insurance may range from $75 to $800 depending on your type of car, deductibles, and where you live; a resident of a big metropolitan city might have higher comprehensive insurance costs than someone who lives in a small town, because the risk of theft is much higher there. As with collision coverage, you may want to do without comprehensive insurance if your car is quite old or in bad shape and would cost more to repair than its book value.

NO-FAULT INSURANCE

You may have witnessed the following scenario on an old TV courtroom drama, like Perry Mason: two cars collide at an intersection; both drivers emerge from their vehicles, fuming at the damage to their cars, but appearing, otherwise, unharmed; they exchange information, and appear to go on their not-so-merry ways. The next scene is a courtroom; one driver enters, wearing a neck brace, propped by a cane, and claiming everything from whiplash to irreparable mental anguish. Trailing behind him are his lawyers; in the long run, after months of costly litigation, it is they who will probably come out happiest while a jury decides the case based in large part on each attorney's "performance."

Such real-life cases—too-often dependent on a jury's subjectivity and the talents of attorneys—were one of the reasons that "no-fault" insurance came into being in the mid-1960s. Created on the same premise as "workmen's compensation" and resembling the "medical payments" coverage in a standard auto insurance package, no-fault insurance enables drivers to collect payments from their own insurance company after an accident, no matter who was at fault.

Sixteen states have adopted some form of no-fault insurance and twelve others are considered "add-ons": they have a no-fault law, but they don't restrict drivers' rights to sue. No two states' insurance laws are exactly alike, and the laws vary primarily in the amounts that insurance companies will pay to clients and the conditions under which drivers can sue one another. Generally, no-fault insurance covers only bodily injury caused to drivers and passengers involved in accidents in "no-fault" states. (Michigan, generally considered to have the most comprehensive no-fault law, is the only state that also requires insurance companies to pay for damages to property —including automobile damages.)

Generally, no-fault laws reduce drivers' worries of being sued after an accident, and usually insurance payments are made more rapidly and efficiently than in non-no-fault states. Also, no-fault laws generally lower auto insurance premiums by doing away with possibilities of costly litigation.

By living in a no-fault state, however, you may be giving up your right to sue (unless you live in one of the "add-on" no-fault states). The situations in which you can sue vary from state to state and usually depend on the seriousness of your injuries. All states, including no-fault and non-no-fault states, will allow your estate or survivors to sue if you are killed in an auto accident.

The following states and territories currently carry some form of no-fault insurance:

Colorado	Michigan
Connecticut	Minnesota
District of Columbia	New Jersey
Florida	New York
Georgia	North Dakota
Hawaii	Puerto Rico
Kansas	Utah
Kentucky	U.S. Virgin Islands
Massachusetts	

The following are currently "add-on" no-fault states:

Arkansas	South Carolina
Delaware	South Dakota
Maryland	Texas
New Hampshire	Virginia
Oregon	Washington
Pennsylvania	Wisconsin

GETTING THE COVERAGE YOU NEED AT THE BEST POSSIBLE PRICE

Insurance, by its very nature, should provide you with a little peace of mind: the simple comforting idea that if your car is wrecked in an accident—or if you total someone else's car—you won't be left penniless in order to pay for damages. But, at a time when auto insurance rates are rising ever higher so that three or four years of coverage can total up to be more than the cost of the car itself, your peace of mind can be transformed into a cause for great concern over whether you'll be able to make your premium payments or not.

To get the best value for your insurance dollar, it's vitally important to shop around carefully. Any two insurance companies could offer you the exact same auto insurance package, but their costs could differ by hundreds of dollars.

Also, carefully compare the costs of what you're paying

against the value of what you're getting. For instance, it's generally advisable to get more liability insurance than the minimum amount required by your state. The difference in your premium could be just a few dollars, but the difference in the coverage you get could be very significant. If your state requires you to have only $20,000 in bodily injury liability insurance, for example, and you cause serious injuries to a driver and three passengers, chances are that $20,000 won't cover the medical costs for even one of those people—and the rest of the money will have to come straight from your pocket. However, if you buy coverage up to $100,000, chances are your insurance company could cover the medical bills for all those people. Remember that liability insurance protects your *assets*, not yourself. The richer you are, the more you have to lose, and the more liability insurance you will want and be able to afford.

Suggestions When Buying Auto Insurance

□   **CHECK THE AUTO INSURANCE LAWS OF YOUR STATE** (particularly if you live in a no-fault state) to see what coverage you are required to buy.

□   **KEEP NOTE OF THE BOOK VALUE OF YOUR CAR:** As your car ages, its value decreases; and as explained earlier in this chapter, you may want to lessen—or to eliminate—your collision coverage. Your library, local banks, or insurance offices should carry what is known colloquially as "The Blue Books." The National Automobile Dealers Association (NADA) is one such publisher of these widely used references. One of their books covers cars of the previous seven model years; the other, cars from eight to seventeen years old. "The Blue Books" will list the typical value of your make of car at different ages, and it's worthwhile to check it from time to time to see if what you're paying for collision coverage is more than the value of the car itself.

□   **CONSIDER WHERE YOU LIVE:** Do you live in an area of high crime? Of harsh weather? Do you usually park your car outdoors rather than in a protected garage? If the answers to these questions are "yes," you'll want to be well covered with comprehensive insurance—the kind that protects you from outside dangers such as floods, theft, and vandalism to your car. Conversely, if you move to a safer area, or if suddenly you have access to a garage, you may want to cut back on this coverage.

☐ **HOW DO YOU USE YOUR CAR?** If you use your car to commute to work everyday, you may want to consider buying certain insurance options—such as use of a rental car while your car is being repaired. Do you carpool? If so, you may want to get extra medical payments insurance to cover non-family members who often may be in your car. Do you use your car just on weekends? If so, your car may be in better shape than the typical value of your car's description in the Blue Book and you may want to hold onto your collision and comprehensive insurance longer than if your car were more damaged.

☐ **WHAT'S COVERED BY YOUR OTHER KINDS OF POLICIES?** You should always compare your auto insurance policy to your health insurance policy to make sure you're not duplicating coverages. For instance, you may be well covered for lost wages during an injury with your medical disability insurance and you may not need wage loss insurance in addition (though no-fault state residents are required to have wage loss insurance). Also, if you belong to an auto club, review what services your membership entitles you to, such as the cost of having your car towed. It would be a waste of money to duplicate this option in your auto insurance plan.

☐ **BALANCING DEDUCTIBLES AGAINST HIGHER PREMIUMS:** In many cases, you can hold down the cost of collision and comprehensive insurance by opting for high "deductibles" (the amount you agree to pay up to before the insurance company will reimburse you for damage costs). The amount you get back after an accident will be less than if your deductible were lower, but your lower year-round cost can more than compensate.

☐ **LOOK INTO DISCOUNTS FOR WHICH YOU MAY QUALIFY:**
There are many details that can hold down the costs of your
auto premiums. Here are some:

Good health habits: Many insurance companies give discounts
to clients who don't smoke or drink alcohol with the idea that
they are less likely to be distracted or impaired while in the
driver's seat. Generally, a concern for one's good health infers
that the person is responsible in other areas of life as well.

How many insurance policies you hold with the same company: Generally, if you have many cars in one family, it's cheaper to have
them all covered by the same insurance policy.

The "track" record of your car: Small cars will tend to cause less
damage in an accident than large ones, though large ones generally will be less damaged. Some cars (luxury or sports cars,
particularly) are more likely to be stolen than other cars, and
insurance costs will be higher for those. If you're buying a new
car and are concerned about high insurance rates, inquire
about the car's claims-loss history before you visit a new car
dealer.

Being a good student: Some insurance companies will offer discounts to high school and college honor students, and/or to
people of any age who have completed a defensive driving
course and/or a driver education course.

Auto-theft devices: Devices such as alarms and sophisticated
locks act as deterrents to would-be thieves and they will enti-
tle you to a discount on insurance with some companies.

Being female: Women are involved in fewer car accidents than
men and therefore qualify for discounts with many insurance
agencies.

Age and marital status: Many companies offer senior citizen
discounts and some offer discounts if you're married, simply
because married people generally have better driving records

than single people. Also, once you are twenty-five years old, many companies will lower your premium; you're no longer in the highest-risk category.

As with any kind of policy, the irony of buying auto insurance is that year after year you spend lots of money on something that you hope you never have to use. But there's comfort in knowing that you're prepared in case of emergency, and that should certainly be significant reassurance.

Maintenance Timetable

DAILY

□ Before getting in your car, look at your headlights and tail-lights; are they covered with mud (or snow, in winter)? If so, your lights will be significantly dimmed. Clean them off, if necessary. Also keep your eye out for nicks in the car's body.

□ Every time you get in your car, adjust mirrors, both rear-view and side view, and make sure your seat is adjusted to a position from which you can easily reach the steering wheel and accelerator and brake pedals.

□ When you start up your engine, listen for any unusual sounds; watch the dashboard closely to make sure that all the lights that *should* go on, do. Also, watch for warning lights (such as those indicating you're low on gas or that oil is not being pumped through the engine).

□ Make sure all seat belts are working. The best way to do this is to wear yours and encourage passengers to do the same.

WEEKLY

□ Check all fluid levels—oil; radiator coolant; battery water (if you don't have a maintenance-free battery); battery electrolyte indicator (if you do have a maintenance-free battery); windshield washer fluid, brakes, power steering, transmission.

☐ Check tire pressure, including the spare.

☐ Make sure taillights, back-up lights, headlights, and directional signals are working properly.

☐ Test that windshield wipers aren't streaking.

☐ Wash your car and clean out loose papers and trash.

MONTHLY
☐ Check tire treads for wear: if tread depth is 1/16th of an inch or less, or tread-wear indicator bars are clearly visible, replace the tire.

☐ Check belts for proper tension and replace those that are frayed, excessively shiny, or loose.

☐ Check hoses for leaks and wear and to make sure that all connections are tight. Replace cracked or broken hoses.

☐ Check exhaust system for leaks and rust, and check the floor of your car for holes.

☐ Check battery for corrosion of battery terminals and check cables for cracks, corrosion, or tightness.

☐ Check brakes by noting if they stop efficiently when you apply the brake pedal at 25 mph; take note if the car pulls to one side, or if you hear any unusual noises.

☐ Check shock absorbers by pushing down on the front— and rear—bumpers; if the car bounces twice or more, have shock absorbers replaced.

TRIANNUALLY
☐ Have a complete oil change (including replacing the oil filter) and lube job, if necessary, every four months, or every 3,000 miles, whichever comes first.

SEMIANNUALLY

☐ Replace windshield wipers.

☐ Rotate tires.

☐ Have a professional tune-up if you've gone 12,000 miles by mid-year.

☐ Wax your car.

ANNUALLY

☐ Have your tires' balance and alignment checked.

☐ Have a professional tune-up, if you haven't already done so.

☐ Replace the air filter, if you haven't already done so.

☐ Have brakes thoroughly examined.

☐ Have alternator, voltage regulator, and battery tested to make sure they all function properly.

☐ Have muffler, catalytic converter, and exhaust pipes checked for loose connections and corrosion.

☐ Have chassis examined for bent, cracked, or loose components.

☐ Have steering adjusted, if necessary.

BIANNUALLY

☐ Flush out old radiator coolant, if it looks discolored, and replace with fresh coolant.

Glossary

AAA: Abbreviation for "American Automobile Association."

Accessory: Any part of the automobile that is not integral to the actual running of the vehicle, including but not limited to the radio, air conditioner, sunroof, etc.

ADM: Abbreviation for "Additional Dealer Markup." See also "ADP."

ADP: Abbreviation for term "Additional Dealer Profit" found on dealers' stickers on new cars. These stickers are supplementary to the manufacturer's stickers and indicate that the sale price of the car has been marked up from the manufacturer's suggested retail price. See also "ADM."

Air filter: Device located in the big metal box in the engine compartment that traps dirt and dust in the air entering the engine.

Alternator: Device that generates electricity to keep the battery charged.

Antifreeze: Ethylene-glycol chemical with a very low freezing point that is mixed with anti-corrosives. Usually mixed in a 50/50 combination with water to form the typical engine coolant.

Anti-lacerative windshield: Windshield that has a thin coating of plastic on the inside surface to protect passengers' heads from shattered glass in the event of an accident.

Antilock brakes: Computer control that regulates the hydraulic pressure applied to each wheel's brake, preventing it from "locking up" and stopping all rotation.

ASE or NIASE: Abbreviation for "National Institute of Automotive Service Excellence," an auto industry group that certifies the competency of automotive technicians in eight different categories of repair.

AUTOCAP: Acronym for "Automobile Consumer Action Program," an arbitration program to help consumers resolve automotive complaint problems, established and run by the National Automobile Dealers Association.

Autoline: Division of the Council of Better Business Bureaus, designed to help consumers resolve automotive complaint disputes.

Axle: Metal rod attached to the rear wheels, transmitting energy from the differential to make the wheels spin.

Battery: Device that stores electricity, generated by the alternator, in chemical form.

Battery terminals: "Negative" and "positive" knobs atop the battery to which you attach the booster cables during a jump-start.

Bearing: Device that allows two parts to slide or rotate with minimum friction and wear, while still retaining their positions accurately.

Belts: On tires, this term refers to an additional layer of material (often steel) that goes over the plies and under the treads of tires. In other parts of the car, belts are used to drive different mechanisms, such as the air conditioner, radiator fan, etc.

Bias-ply tires: Tires whose plies are laid out in an angled fashion.

Blue Books: Colloquial term for books published by the National Automobile Dealer's Association and others that list the current value of used cars. Available in banks and libraries, these books are helpful in determining the selling price of a used car and in deciding the coverage of certain types of auto insurance necessary for a particular car.

Booster cable (jumper cable): Cable used to conduct electricity from one car battery to another in a "jump-start" procedure.

Brake: Device that slows and stops the wheels from turning, hence, reducing or putting an end to a car's motion.

Caliper: Part of the disc brake, arching over the edge of the disc, that supports the brake pads and that, under hydraulic pressure, forces them against the disc, stopping the disc—and the wheel.

Camber: The lean angle of a car's wheels, either in or out at the top, when viewed from the front of the car.

Camshaft: Device within the four-stroke engine that precisely controls the opening and closing of the valves.

Carburetor: Mechanism of the fuel system that regulates the air/fuel mixture into the engine cylinders.

Caster: Angle of the turning axes of the front wheels as they are moved by the steering wheel.

Catalytic converter: Device located in the exhaust system that chemically changes carbon monoxide and hydrocarbons produced in the engine into less polluting and less hazardous carbon dioxide and water.

Choke: Device in the carburetor that restricts air flow into the carburetor when the engine is cold, thus giving the engine a greater proportion of fuel in the mixture for easier starting and better warm-up operation.

Clutch: Device that temporarily disconnects the engine from the manual transmission to allow gears to be shifted in the transmission.

Collision insurance: Insurance that covers the cost of repairs to a policyholder's car in case of a crash.

Comprehensive insurance: Insurance that covers the cost of damages to a policyholder's car caused by circumstances other than an accident involving another car, person, or fixed object.

Coolant: See "Antifreeze."

Cooling system: One of a car's twelve major systems, designed to circulate an antifreeze/water mixture throughout the engine to absorb heat and prevent overheating.

Crankcase: Lower part of the engine block that supports the crankshaft, and at the bottom of which is the oil pan.

Crankshaft: Main shaft in the engine that transmits power from the pistons to the transmission.

Crash test: Specific procedures that evaluate the performance of a car and its safety features in a controlled "accident," for compliance with federal motor vehicle safety standards.

Cruise control: Accessory that keeps your car moving at a constant speed without your foot on the accelerator pedal, until you apply the brake pedal; usually used in long highway drives.

Cylinders: Metal column-shaped spaces in your engine that house the pistons where the four-stroke engine process takes place.

Dealer cost: Amount of money an automobile dealer pays the manufacturer for a new car, which he will then sell from his showroom at a higher price.

Diesel engine: Fuel-injected system without a carburetor that burns diesel fuel instead of gasoline.

Diesel fuel: Heavy mineral oil used as fuel in diesel engines.

Differential: Device that allows the drive wheels of a car to rotate at different speeds, which occurs in turning a corner.

Dipsticks: Metal rods that jut out of containers that hold fluids such as oil, power steering fluid, and transmission fluid—and with which one can measure the level of the fluid in that container.

Disc brake: Brake in which brake pads are pressed against both sides of a rotating metal plate.

Distributor: Part of the ignition system that sends high voltage to each spark plug in turn at the correct time.

Driveshaft: Steel tube that runs the longitudinal axis of the car, transmitting power from the transmission to the differential.

Drum brake: Brake in which brake shoes are pressed against the inside perimeter of a rotating metal cylinder.

EPA: Abbreviation for "Environmental Protection Agency."

Exhaust manifold: Device that collects exhaust gases leaving the individual engine cylinders and carries them to the exhaust pipe.

Exhaust pipe: Metal tube that carries exhaust gases from the exhaust manifold to the catalytic converter, or to the muffler.

Filter: One of usually six different devices that prevents contaminants from entering automobile components.

Firewall: Panel that separates the engine compartment from the
passenger compartment.

Flooding: Situation in which too much fuel is fed into the engine
so that it won't start.

Flywheel: Rotating metal plate on the end of the crankshaft to
which the clutch is connected.

Front-wheel drive: A process in which power is carried from the
transmission directly to the differential, which then splits
the energy between the two front (or "driving") wheels,
providing good traction.

Fuel efficiency: Term describing an engine's use of fuel; expressed
in miles per gallon and indicating an average distance that
a car can travel on one gallon of fuel. (Efficiency is better
in constant-speed highway driving than in stop-and-go
city driving.)

Fuel filter: Device connected to the fuel line that removes dirt
particles from the gasoline before it is sent into the carburetor and eventually the engine.

Fuel injector: Device on all diesel-run vehicles and some gasoline
automobiles that squirts fuel directly into the engine,
eliminating the need for a carburetor.

Fuel line: Steel tubing through which gasoline is pumped from
the gas tank to the fuel filter.

Fuel pump: Device that moves fuel from your gas tank through
the fuel line to the engine.

Gear: Device for transferring motion, used in transmission and
steering systems.

Handling: Overall feel of the car as it is being driven, including
the ease with which it accelerates, turns, brakes, etc.

Hose: Rubber tubing that runs from the radiator through the
engine and back again, carrying coolant to and from the
radiator.

Hose clamps: Adjustable metal rings that secure a hose onto its
connecting component, preventing leaks and "snap-offs."

Hydroplaning: Situation in which a car's tires ride up on a puddle's surface so that the water forms a layer between the

wheels and the ground, as if the wheels were "water skiing" on the puddle, out of contact with the road.

Ignition: System that provides the electrical charge to ignite the fuel/air mixture inside the engine to start the car.

Jack: Device used to raise—and hold—a car above the ground while a flat tire is being changed.

Jump-start: Process in which a "dead" battery receives an electrical charge from a working car battery through the use of booster cables.

Jumper cables: See "Booster cable."

Liability insurance: Insurance that covers the cost of medical payments or damages to personal property of persons involved in an accident other than the insurance policyholder.

Lubrication system: System in a car that circulates oil to all engine parts to cushion and cool parts.

Lug nuts: Metal nuts that secure the tires onto the axle.

Manifold: Device attached to the engine that has several openings through which exhaust gases leave the engine and are transported through the rest of the exhaust system out the tailpipe.

Master cylinder: Device controlled by the brake pedal that creates and distributes hydraulic pressure to each wheel brake.

MPG: Abbreviation for "Miles Per Gallon."

Muffler: Device located in the exhaust system that absorbs the noises produced by exploding gases in the engine.

NADA: Abbreviation for "National Automobile Dealers Association."

Odometer: Digital indicator on the dashboard that counts the distance in miles that a car travels.

Oil pan: Reservoir of oil at the bottom of the engine that supplies the lubrication system's oil pump.

Options: Features of new cars whose costs are not included in the basic retail price of the car.

PCV valve: Abbreviation for the "Positive crankcase ventilation" valve that recycles exhaust gases escaped inside into the engine, rather than out the exhaust pipe.

Performance: Term describing the overall operation of a vehicle.

Petcock: Faucet-like drain at the base of the radiator.

Pick-Up: Colloquial term describing the ease with which a car can increase its speed, either from a stop or a constant speed.

Piston: Metal part in each cylinder that moves up and down during the four-stroke process and transmits power through the connecting rods to the crankshaft.

Pitman arm: Short pivoting bar that connects the steering gear to other links to turn the wheels right or left.

Positive crankcase ventilation system: See "PCV valve."

Premium: The periodic fee car owners pay for insurance coverage.

PSI: Abbreviation for "Pound Per Square Inch," a measure of pressure inside a container.

Rack-and-pinion steering: Steering system in which the steering column shaft connects through a small round gear (pinion) to a notched bar (rack) running perpendicular to the wheels.

Radial tire: Belted tire whose plies are arranged on a line through the center of rotation of the tire.

Radiator: Device that reduces the temperature of the coolant before it is circulated back through the engine.

Rear-wheel drive: Process in which the driveshaft transmits power from the engine to the differential, which in turn transmits the power to each of the rear wheels of the car.

Rotor: Device that conducts electricity inside the distributor to the individual ignition wires. Also, another name for the "disc" part of a disc brake.

Shock absorber: Mechanism near each wheel that reduces the vibration of the spring after the wheel passes over a bump.

Solenoid: Electrically operated device that moves the starter drive gear into and out of engagement with the flywheel.

Spark plug: Device in each engine cylinder that ignites the air/fuel mixture within it.

Speedometer: Gauge on the dashboard that indicates the speed of the car in miles per hour.

Springs: As part of the suspension system, the springs support the bulk of the weight of the automobile and help to absorb the impact of bumps in the road.

Squeegee: To smooth, press, or wipe free of water, usually using a rubber device.

Starter motor: Device operated by a solenoid that turns the flywheel, thus causing the engine pistons to move up and down, prior to the engine being able to run on its own.

Suspension system: Arrangement of springs, shock absorbers, and bearings that keeps the car body properly suspended over the wheels.

Tachometer: Gauge on some automobile dashboards that indicates engine speed in rpm (revolutions per minute).

Tailpipe: Last section of the exhaust pipe through which engine exhaust gases are expelled into the air.

Test drive: Drive that a buyer takes in an automobile he or she is considering purchasing; also, a drive an owner might take *before* paying for a repair to ensure that a problem has been corrected.

Thermostat: Device that regulates the coolant temperature in the engine.

Toe angle: Angle that the tires on one end of a car make with each other, when viewed from above the car.

Transmission: System of gears that transfers engine power to the drive wheels.

Tread-wear bars: Narrow strips of smooth rubber that appear on a tire when its tread is worn to a dangerous point.

Tune-up: Regular maintenance "checkup" during which the mechanic checks all parts of the ignition system.

Turbocharger: Optional device on some cars that forces extra air into engine cylinders to increase engine power.

Vapor canister: Storage container that collects gasoline vapors from the fuel system and returns them to the carburetor.

VIN: Abbreviation for the "Vehicle Identification Number" that's assigned to a car when it's registered.

Voltage regulator: Device that controls the amount of electricity generated in the alternator, according to the changing needs of the battery.

Warranty: Contract provided by an auto manufacturer to a buyer, stating that the manufacturer will cover costs of specified repairs to the car for a specified amount of time.

Water pump: Device that circulates coolant from the radiator to
  the engine.
Wheel cylinder: In drum brakes, the device that forces the brake
  shoes, under hydraulic pressure, against the sides of the
  drum.

Index